# ANSWER CALL TO DUTY:

## SAVING CUSTER, HEROISM AT GETTYSBURG, POWS AND OTHER STORIES OF MICHIGAN'S SMALL TOWN SOLDIERS IN THE CIVIL WAR

### RICK LIBLONG

John Heiser
2010

ARBUTUS PRESS

TRAVERSE CITY, MICHIGAN

# ANSWERING THE CALL TO DUTY:
## SAVING CUSTER HEROISM AT GETTYSBURG, POWS OTHER STORIES OF MICHIGAN'S SMALL TOWN SOLDIERS IN THE CIVIL WAR

Author's royalties will be donated to the Richard P. and Susan R. Liblong Endowed Scholarship for Communication Arts and Sciences at Michigan State University.

The information in this book is true and complete as to the best of our knowledge. It is offered without guarantee on the part of the author or Arbutus Press. The author and Arbutus Press disclaim all liability in connection with the use of this book.

ISBN 978-1-933926-29-2

Cover image: Ron Lesser, *Custer's Gallant Charge at Gettysburg*
Interior sketch: John Heiser, *Norvell Churchill Saving General Custer*

Manufactured in the United States of America

ARBUTUS PRESS
TRAVERSE CITY, MICHIGAN
INFO@ARBUTUSPRESS.COM
WWW.ARBUTUSPRESS.COM

# Contents

# DEDICATION

## TO SUE
## MY PERFECT, SWEET PRINCESS

and

## TO THE PEOPLE OF ALMONT, LAPEER COUNTY
### AND THE STATE OF MICHIGAN

**The Michigan Coat of Arms during the Civil War**

# INTRODUCTION

The guns, of course, are silent now. The killing fields are gentle, pastoral lands made into national parks where tourists rather than warriors mingle. One hundred and fifty years ago, however, these same peaceful lands witnessed the most horrific fury and carnage ever seen on the North American continent.

In the last century and a half, more than 50,000 books have been written about the American Civil War. Most of them are about one or more specific generals or the major battles, war strategy, etc. This book is not meant to be an all inclusive Civil War book. It is a portrait of some Michiganians and the war told by concentrating on one county and one small village and township that are typical of the many other areas that sent their sons to the army to fight to save the Union. Some of these men fought under the infamous George Armstrong Custer. One of them saved Custer's life. Many fought at Antietam, Gettysburg, Gaines Mill, Trevilian Station, Chattanooga, Atlanta, Chickamauga, the Wilderness, Chancellorsville, Cold Harbor, Cedar Creek, Winchester and many other battles. Some were there when General Robert E. Lee surrendered to General Ulysses S. Grant at Appomattox Court House.

Lapeer County and Almont in Michigan's "Thumb," sent more than 1,500 men to rally around the flag, the Constitution and to help preserve the United States of America. This is the story of some of them.

I have chosen Lapeer County and Almont to profile in this book because I believe they were representative of the counties and hundreds of small towns all across Michigan...and it's where I grew up. In addition, I have included five brothers from adjacent St. Clair County because the grandson of one of them was my neighbor.

The State of Michigan, while a long way from the battle front, eventually sent 31 infantry regiments, 11 cavalry regiments, 1 artillery regiment consisting of 12 batteries, 1 unit of engineers and 1 of sharpshooters.

In all, Michigan sent nearly 90,000 men, one quarter of the male population, one half of the military age men, into battle (and at least one woman, Sarah Edmunds from Flint, who posed as "Frank Thompson"). Nearly 1,300 Michigan men served in other states' units as well and 600 joined the U. S. Navy. A large majority of the men came from farms, small towns and villages all over the state. Most were white men with many of them being recent immigrants who barley spoke English. Approximately 1,600 were African Americans and at least 145 were Native Americans.

More than 14,500 Michiganians paid the ultimate price, one of every six who served. There were 4,448 killed in action and 10,305 who died of other causes. Some were missing in action. Sixty-seven were awarded the Medal of Honor including three from Lapeer County.

Sixteen Almonters were killed in battle, 134 from the county. Nineteen Almonters died of disease or other causes along with the nearly 200 from the county.

Disease was a major killer during the war. One soldier in a Michigan Infantry Regiment noted that about 30 men of his unit had died of disease while none had been killed by the Confederates.

What follows are profiles of rural Michigan, Lapeer County and Almont before and during the war as well as the story of Almont's growth after the war.

The heart of this book, however, is really the stories of individual men who left their homes and families to join the struggle to preserve the Union. I chose these men for their different backgrounds, age, rank and professions and their experiences in the War Between the States.

They answered the call to duty.

Rick Liblong / Winter, 2010

# FOREWORD

*We have shared the incommunicable experience of war. We felt, we still feel, the passion of life to its top. In our youths, our hearts were touched by fire. Oliver Wendell Holmes*

Growing up as a young boy in Royal Oak, a northern suburb of Detroit, I was very fortunate to have my maternal grandfather, Harrison David Churchill, living with our family. He was a wonderful grandfather who had lived through much tougher times and was willing to share his life stories and experiences with me.

I learned at a very early age that my great-grandfather, Norvell Churchill, had saved General Custer's life in the Civil War and the sabre he had used to block a confederate soldier's blow, attempting to end the life of the young golden-haired general, was still in the family. The hash mark in the blade was still visible. It would take another 55 years before I was actually able to hold this sabre and see the mark, but it was well worth the wait. What pride I had that I actually had a "hero" for a relative.

In this book, Rick Liblong eloquently and realistically presents many of the actual heroes of the Lapeer County and Almont, Michigan area where my great-grandfather resided. He shows the hardships these young soldiers endured along with those of the families that many of them had left behind. I say 'actual heroes' because almost each and every one of them performed the duties they were assigned to save and reunite this wonderful country in which we are so blessed to live. They did so while believing it would be only for a short period of time. It turned out to be many years for most and far too many of them were never able to return to their small home towns, their farms and more importantly to their families.

The Civil War has often been called the 'war of brother against brother' and was a critical test of our nation—an event of great turmoil for all of the people in the United States. There were thousands of small towns throughout our country, many similar to Almont, where young men and civilians were asked to serve their country and to make sacrifices far beyond those most of us reading this book will ever be called on to make. The fine citizens of Lapeer County and Almont who responded and served, fought valiantly and with honor. Some perished but most were fortunate enough to return home, and with their descendants, continue to make that area the growing place it is today.

I hope you enjoy reading this fine piece of work that Rick Liblong has created and that it helps you realize that there is more to true heroism than just one action taken by an individual, as a result of being in a certain place at the right time.

RICHARD J. WEBB
Winter, 2010

**Richard J. Webb with Norvell Churchill's sabre and "General Custer"**
**(Steve Alexander) (Courtesy Webb Family)**

# CHAPTER ONE

Rural Michigan in the War

"Thank God for Michigan!" That's what President Abraham Lincoln is reported to have said when the 1st Michigan Infantry entered Washington and became the first western military unit to answer his call for troops to put down the rebellion of Southern states.

After the firing on Fort Sumter on April 12, 1861, President Lincoln called for volunteers to quell the rebellion.

## HARPER'S WEEKLY.

### SATURDAY, APRIL 27, 1861.

*By the President of the United States:*

**A PROCLAMATION.**

Whereas, The laws of the United States have been for some time past and now are opposed, and the execution thereof obstructed, in the States of South Carolina, Georgia, Alabama, Florida, Mississippi, Louisiana, and Texas, by combinations too powerful to be suppressed by the ordinary course of judicial proceedings, or by the powers vested in the Marshals by law :

Now, therefore, I, ABRAHAM LINCOLN, President of the United States, in virtue of the power in me vested by the Constitution and the laws, have thought fit to call forth, and hereby do call forth, the Militia of the several States of the Union, to the aggregate number of 75,000, in order to suppress said combinations, and to cause the laws to be duly executed. The details for this object will be immediately communicated to the State authorities through the War Department.

I appeal to all loyal citizens to favor, facilitate and aid this effort to maintain the honor, the integrity, and the existence of our National Union and the perpetuity of popular government, and to redress wrongs already long enough endured...

In witness whereof, I have hereunto set my hand, and caused the seal of the United States to be affixed.

Done at the City of Washington, this fifteenth day of April, in the year of our Lord one thousand eight hundred and sixty-one, and of the independence of the United States the eighty-fifth.

ABRAHAM LINCOLM

BY THE PRESIDENT.

WILLIAM H. SEWARD

SECRETARY OF STATE.


The United States Army only had 16,000 regulars in 1861 and more than 300 officers resigned and joined the Confederacy. So Lincoln had no choice but to call for more men.

Michigan, from the Indian word "Mishigama," meaning "large lake" or "large water," became the 26th State on January 26, 1837. By 1860 the state's population had grown to 749,113. Its two peninsulas consisted of 87 counties, more than 1,200 townships and 600 cities, towns and villages. There are now 83 counties.

Michigan was teeming with tall timber stands and for years the lumbering business thrived. Lush farmland was also abundant in the state so farming was a leading industry. Being surrounded by the Great Lakes and with miles and miles of fresh water rivers and streams, the fishing industry was big as well, as was Great Lakes shipping. There was some manufacturing of durable goods such as buggies but much of the Industrial Revolution that would put the world on wheels and transform Michigan and the country was still a few years off.

Before the war Michigan was very Republican, was very pro-Union and very anti-slavery. The Republican Party was founded in Jackson, Michigan in 1856.

The state was a major route on the Underground Railroad for escaped or freed slaves on their way to Canada across the St. Clair and

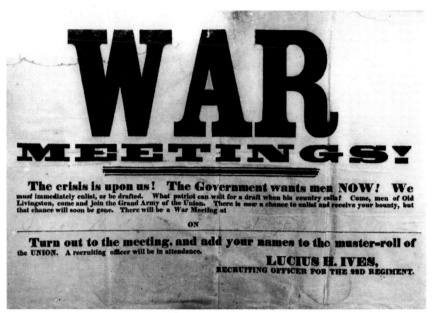

War poster for Livingston County (Michigan State Archives)

Detroit Rivers. One of many stops along the way, for example, was The White Horse Inn built in 1850 in Metamora, Lapeer County.

Nearly every Governor and his Adjutant General responded to Lincoln's call including Michigan. Newly elected Republican Governor Austin Blair, a strong opponent of slavery and secession, called for ten companies of troops to be raised. By the end of the war, Michigan had raised 31 infantry regiments, 11 cavalry regiments, 14 artillery batteries, 1 sharpshooter unit and 1 engineer unit.

Each state had an Adjutant General usually appointed by and reporting to the Governor. In Michigan's case, Governor Blair appointed John R. Robertson of Detroit to the post in March, 1861 where he served throughout the war until 1867. Mr. Robertson had emigrated from England to the United States specifically to join the U.S. Army which he did in 1833 in the Wisconsin Territory. He came with his regiment to Detroit as Quartermaster in 1840 and after his service he joined a merchant firm in Detroit.

The Governor would get requests for troops from the President through the Secretary of War. The Adjutant General, on behalf of the Governor, was responsible for carrying out the Governor's request for troops. He supervised the many enlistment centers in the state and made sure that the enlistees were paid, outfitted and provided with transportation.

Across the state the recruiting continued. Ottawa County, bordering Lake Michigan on the western shore of the state, sent 1,547 men to the Union Army. Bay County, only four years old in 1861, which borders Saginaw Bay (between the Thumb and Palm of the Lower Peninsula), lost more than 60 of its sons in the war. Berrien County, in the southwest corner of the Lower Peninsula, contributed more than 3,000 men out of a population of just over 20,000. The tiny villages of Saugatuck and Douglas on Lake Michigan in Allegan County sent eight men, all of whom survived the war.

The quotas filled by rural areas of Michigan were filled, of course, with individuals.

Oloff Carlson, 40, enlisted in Company K of the 28th Michigan Infantry at Houghton in the U. P. The 28th engaged the rebels at Wise Forks, N.C., taking more than 300 prisoners. He served until June 5, 1866.

Sherman A. Rhodes, age 20, came from Saginaw County and enlisted in the 3rd Michigan Cavalry, which was engaged in more than 25 skirmishes and battles, including Corinth, Mississippi, and lost 25 men killed in action.

From Sault Ste. Marie in the U.P. came Joseph Kemp to Company D, 5th Michigan Infantry. First Sergeant Kemp was awarded the Medal of Honor for capturing the flag of the 31st North Carolina at the Battle of the Wilderness in Virginia.

Entering service in the 26th Michigan Infantry from Muskegon was Alexander J. McHale, 22, who was also awarded the Medal of Honor for heroism at Spotsylvania Courthouse, Virginia.

Garrett Graveraet joined the 1st Michigan Sharpshooters in Little Traverse (now Harbor Springs). Part Native American, he recruited Native Americans for the 1st from Northport, Omena, Cross Village, Bear River, Charlevoix, Burt and the Mackinac region. They saw action in Virginia including Cold Harbor and Petersburg. Unfortunately, Second Lieutenant Graveraet died from wounds received at Petersburg.

Elias Browning of Detroit enlisted in Company G, 24th Michigan Infantry as a musician July 24, 1862 for 3 years at age 18. The 24th was part of the famous Iron Brigade and suffered the most casualties of any regiment at Gettysburg. Private Browning was killed in action at Gettysburg July 1, 1863 and is buried in the National Cemetery, Gettysburg, PA.

William Koepfgen joined the 22nd Infantry from Port Huron while his brother, John, came from Wales. William was wounded at Chickamauga while carrying the regimental flag, taken prisoner and later exchanged for a Confederate prisoner. John died of disease in Nashville, Tennessee in 1863.

Many soldiers continued to serve Michigan as civilians after the war. From Jackson came Austin Blair, who served as Governor of Michigan during the Civil War.

Russell Alger from Grand Rapids helped organize and command several Michigan Cavalry units and later from 1902 to 1907 was Governor. He went on to become Secretary of War and a U.S. Senator.

From the farm in St. Clair County to Colonel of the 23rd Michigan Infantry, David Jerome was later elected Governor in 1880.

And Moses Wisner, Governor from 1859 to 1861, helped raise and command the 22nd Michigan Infantry. He was from Lapeer. Unfortunately, on the regiment's deployment in 1862, Wisner died of Typhoid Fever in Lexington, Kentucky.

And so it was all across the Wolverine State as man after man enlisted to

Governor Russell Alger (Lincoln Library, Chicago, IL)

fight for the Union. Their farms and businesses were left to be run by families and friends.

The civilians left behind contributed money, made war material, sewed clothes, grew and shipped food and wrote letters to their soldiers as a reminder of home. It was a total war effort by nearly every Michiganian as everyone was touched in some way by the conflict.

The same can be said for every other state as the pattern played out all across the North and South in small town after small town. And then came the job of becoming a soldier.

Once the men had enlisted they were mustered into the service in one of 21 cities and towns and went to training camps scattered around Michigan. The main camp was at *Fort Wayne* in Detroit. Among the others were *Camp Backus* and *Camp Lyon* in Detroit, *Fort Gratiot* in Port Huron, *Camp Butler* in Mt. Clemens, *Camp Williams* in Adrian and other facilities in Pontiac and Dearborn.

After a few weeks training the regiments were deployed to the war zone. Most of those who would fight in the Eastern Theater embarked by boat from Port Huron or Detroit and sailed to Cleveland

**A Company of the 21st Michigan Infantry in Union service**
**(Brady photo, National Archives)**

15

where they boarded trains for the trip to the battle front. The Western Theater regiments usually left by train from Detroit or Pontiac.

Not all of these 90,000 men were heroes. Far from it. Many of them were scoundrels and cheats, some deserted and some committed grave atrocities. But by and large, all of them honorably answered the call to duty.

# CHAPTER TWO

# A RURAL COUNTY: LAPEER

The first American flag flew over what was to become Michigan in 1796 when the Americans occupied Detroit. An act of Congress on January 11, 1805 stated:

*"that from and after the 30th day of June of that year all this part of Indiana Territory, which lies north of a line drawn east from the southerly bend, or extreme, of Lake Michigan, until it shall intersect Lake Erie, and east of a line drawn from the said southerly bend, through the middle said lake to its northern extremity, and thence due north to the northern boundary of the United States, shall constitute a separate territory, and be called Michigan."*

President Thomas Jefferson appointed General William Hull as Michigan's first territorial governor. In the War of 1812, however, the British retook Michigan but finally on September 10, 1813, after a decisive victory in the Battle of Lake Erie by Commodore Oliver Hazard Perry, Michigan returned to the United States for good.

Counties began to be formed in 1807 with Monroe County as the first and on September 10, 1822 Governor Lewis Cass, under authority of an act of Congress, declared ten new counties. The proclamation read:

*"... shall form a county to be called the county of Lapeer."*

**Lapeer County in Michigan's Thumb**

On January 26, 1837 Congress declared Michigan to *"be one of the United States, and admitted to the Union on an equal footing with the original States, in all respects whatever"* under the leadership of the youngest governor on American history, Stevens T. Mason.

In 1847 the capital of the state moved from Detroit to Lansing. Between 1833 and 1838 a huge immigration took place from the Eastern States to the west and Michigan. The state's population more than doubled in those years. Loans were available and land was $1.25 per acre. Long lines formed at the land office in Flint. The first settler in the county was James Deneen, who moved to what is now Almont Township from Ohio in 1828. Almont is the oldest township in the county.

The population of the county in 1840 was 3,364. By 1860 at the start of the Civil War it was 14,754.

When Lapeer County was first laid out in the Michigan Territory it contained twenty-seven townships. Today there are eighteen. The first election of county officers was not held until 1836 when the following were elected: Samuel Merlin, Sheriff, Noah H. Hart, Clerk, Joseph B. Hart, Treasurer, Caleb Carpenter, Register and Henry M. Look as Judge of Probate.

Lapeer County was, and is, predominantly a rural area with farming as the primary industry. In the 1880 census it is recorded that there were 3,850 farms in the county and 186 manufacturing establishments. The county also had its share of merchants, teachers, lawyers and doctors and as late as 1872 boasted nearly thirty sawmills. From the vast forests of Michigan, these mills made lumber for buildings, shingles for houses, logs for homes, ties for the railroad, bridges, boards for buggies, poles for telegraph lines and anything else that could be made of wood. Lumbering was the largest industry before the forests were cleared.

The Adjutant General, reporting to the Governor, set quotas of recruits for counties to meet. After quotas were set, "war meetings" were held all over Michigan in every township and village. County sheriffs and clerks were usually "recruiting officers." But the state also relied on individual citizens to recruit men for a regiment and then these citizens were appointed as an officer in the unit by the Governor. In addition, provost marshals were appointed by Edwin M. Stanton, Secretary of War to help in the recruiting and emphasizing the draft.

In Lapeer County the sheriffs during the war were Samuel Carpenter (1860-1862), E. R. Emmons (1862-1864) and John B. Sutton (1864-1866). The clerks were Hubbell Loomis (1860-1864) and Jasper Bentley (1864-1874).

Federal, state and local authorities and private donors and organizations alike sometimes provided cash bonuses to enlistees and financial support for their families. "Bounty" amounts fluctuated throughout the war but later they served as incentives for men to avoid the draft.

In a special town meeting in Almont on November 24, 1862, it was voted 231 to 76 to raise the sum of $4,000 as a fund from which to pay bounties to volunteer soldiers under the call of the government for 300,000 men. The payments began early in 1863.

During the Civil War every township in Lapeer County sent troops to the Union Army as did most of the counties and townships in the state. In all, more than 1,500 county men, about 10% of the county's population, served in nearly every regiment of the war. One hundred thirty four were killed in action. More than 200 died from disease or other causes.

Lapeer County native Orlando LeValley was the last surviving Civil War veteran in the state. He passed away in 1947.

The 1st Michigan Cavalry had the most men from Lapeer County, 29, killed in action. The 1st was part of the Michigan Brigade of cavalry (1st, 5th, 6th, 7th) in the Army of the Potomac. The brigade, under its flamboyant commander General George Armstrong Custer, saw action in most of the battles in the Eastern Theater.

Twenty-seven county men who joined the 7th Michigan Infantry, which was engaged in every battle from Bull Run, to Antietam, Fredericksburg, Gettysburg, Petersburg and all the way to Lee's surrender at Appomattox Court House, paid the ultimate price.

The 10th Michigan Infantry, organized in 1862, saw action in the Western Theater of Tennessee, Georgia, North Carolina and Alabama, and lost 20 killed in action from Lapeer County.

And on it went with county men in the 1st Michigan Infantry, 4th Infantry, 5th Infantry, 8th Infantry, 11th Infantry, 13th, 14th, 15th, 16th, 22nd, 26th, and 27th Infantries as well as six cavalry regiments, 2 units of sharpshooters, the 1st Engineers and 1st Light Artillery all giving their lives in combat.

Three Lapeer County men were awarded the nation's highest honor.

**Civil War Medal of Honor**
**(Courtesy of John Heiser, Gettysburg National Military Park)**

George W. Clute, 19, of Marathon, assigned to the 14th Michigan Infantry, Company I, was awarded the Medal of Honor for his bravery at the Battle of Bentonville, North Carolina on March 19, 1865. His citation reads *"In a charge, captured the flag of the 40th North Carolina (C.S.A.), the flag being taken in a personal encounter with an officer who carried and defended it"*. The Medal was awarded to him on August 26, 1898.

Sidney Haight, 17, from Goodland, 1st Michigan Sharpshooters, Company E was awarded the Medal of Honor also. *"The President of the United States of America, in the name of Congress, takes pleasure in presenting the Medal of Honor to Corporal Sidney Haight, United States Army, for extraordinary heroism on 30 July 1864, while serving with Company E, 1st Michigan Sharpshooters, in action at Petersburg, Virginia. Instead of retreating, Corporal Haight remained in the captured works, regardless of his personal safety and exposed to the firing, which he boldly and deliberately returned until the enemy was close upon him."*

Private Frederick Alber, 17th Michigan Infantry, was awarded the Medal of Honor for bravery at Spotsylvania, Virginia on May 12, 1864 for rescuing Lt. Charles H. Todd of his regiment. Alber is buried in Oregon Township.

**author photo**

The brave people of Lapeer County, soldiers and civilians alike, did their part to answer the call to duty.

# CHAPTER THREE

# A TYPICAL SMALL TOWN: ALMONT, MICHIGAN 1860-1865

In the 1860s America was still an agrarian, almost frontier, society. The real industrialization of the nation was still a few years off. There were big cities to be sure, like New York, Philadelphia, Richmond and Boston to name a few. But the vast majority of people lived on farms or in small towns and villages in both the North and the South. Michigan was no exception. Detroit was its largest city with a population of just under 46,000 but there were smaller townships and settlements that played an important part in America's Civil War.

Almont, Michigan, my hometown, is typical of the small towns all over Michigan that sent troops to the Civil War. It was a township and village actually, located approximately 45 miles north of Detroit and when duty called, Almont, along with many other Michigan towns and villages, answered the call.

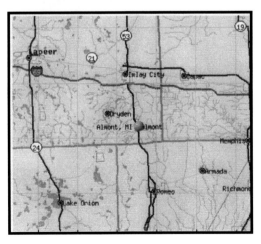

Almont is Michigan's sixth oldest village and many of Almont's sons and daughters have served in all of America's conflicts, including the Civil War, to help keep Michigan and the nation free.

Almont, population about 890 (2,000 in the

township) in the 1860 census, was organized in 1834 before Michigan was admitted to the union and was known by the names of "Bristol" and "Newburg." It was named "Almont" in 1846, probably by James Thompson who came from a region in Scotland where there is still a Hotel Almont.

It was made up of many nationalities including, but not limited to, German, Scottish, Polish, Irish, English and Italian.

The first land purchase in the township dates to 1828.

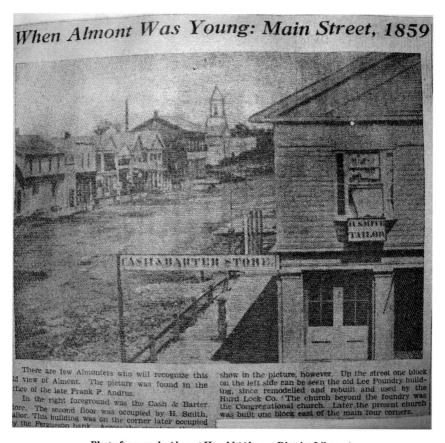

**When Almont Was Young: Main Street, 1859**

There are few Almonters who will recognize this old view of Almont. The picture was found in the office of the late Frank P. Andrus.

In the right foreground was the Cash & Barter store. The second floor was occupied by H. Smith, tailor. This building was on the corner later occupied by the Fergueson bank. Across the show in the picture, however. Up the street one block on the left side can be seen the old Lee Foundry building, since remodelled and rebuilt and used by the Hurd Lock Co. The church beyond the foundry was the Congregational church. Later the present church was built one block east of the main four corners.

**Photo from early Almont Herald (Almont District Library)**

In 1861 the village was about two blocks long and wide with businesses and merchants along each side of Main Street. These included Ami M. Roberts, wagon maker; Gary Goodrich's hotel;

which became the meeting place and social center of the township; general merchant W.W. Taylor; and William Morrison, blacksmith.

Edwin Gould was a liveryman; H. A. Currier, a machinist; H. Taylor, tailor; Joseph Simon, Jr., a carriage maker; Hiram and D.P. Smith were tailors. The village boasted several attorneys, a dry goods store, a tannery, another hotel, four shoe shops, saloons, grist and sawmills, grocery store, three doctors, a harness shop, drug store, foundry, newspaper, four churches and a lamplighter.

National House Hotel, Almont (Almont District Library)

For a small village, Almont was equipped with a good business mix and business was booming. Hitching posts lined both sides of the street with horse watering troughs positioned strategically around the village. Long before paving was invented, a plank road from Detroit through Almont made it easier for Almonters to trade their goods by wagon team since there was no railroad through the village yet. The toll on the plank road was about 50 cents each way and a trip to the Detroit markets by horse or oxen team could take up to three days roundtrip.

In the early 1860s there were five private schools in Almont because, it was said, the people were coming here so fast that the public school could not house the children.

25

It can also be stated that there was a great deal of community involvement and that faith played a very large part of nearly everyone's life. There were several churches of differing denominations.

By far the biggest industry in and around Almont, as well as most small towns in Michigan, was farming. The many farms surrounding the village were blessed with lush land providing nearly every crop and fruit imaginable as well as plenty of livestock. Most of the men who went off to war were farm owners and farm laborers.

While they were in service, the farms were capably run by their wives and family members with an occasional helping hand from a neighbor.

Eveline Churchill, wife of Norvell's brother, Peter (4th Michigan Infantry), wrote the following in a letter to her husband on April 13, 1865:

*"We have six little pigs a week old. They are nice little fellows. How many do you think it will be best to keep? If Lester is not drafted he would like to take our place to work...Norville [sic] says he will put in what oats I have which is 3 bu, Lumis Ives will find seed and put in some oats and the rest somebody would work..."*

The Almont area was a great place to raise a family. A letter from Village President Ripley Shaw, who was moving to Pontiac for different work, was republished in *The Almont Herald* in 1930. It reads in part:

*"...I can't bring this letter to a close without saying something about those who lived there (Almont) at the time. If you met a stranger, you would be safe to call him or her 'Hough' as they occupied much of the territory south and west of the village and were well known as good and upright New England citizens. Then there was that great Scotch Settlement, south and east of town, through Bruce and Berlin; that was a colony to be proud of. I knew them, every one, - the Braidwoods, the Millikins, the Mortons, Jock Muir, Jim Steel, Uncle Jno.*

*Watson, Jno. Hopkins, Adam Watson, the Cochranes, Adam Mackie, the Allens and Taylors and scores of others, all good citizens. Coming back to the village, there were some unique characters: Gary Goodrich, who built the hotel, witty, genial, full of fun, always on hand for a joke. Uncle Daniel Black. A book could easily be written of his witty sayings. It has been my pride to have my family gather here just as long as possible, which was done for many years."*

All four seasons made their annual appearances in Almont. In spring, everyone waited for the snow to melt and for the farmers to get out behind the horse-drawn plows and put in this year's planting.

Summers were moderate. It would occasionally reach 90 degrees, but it was usually in the 70s or low 80s with sunny skies and low humidity. Most years Almont was blessed with an adequate amount of rainfall for a bumper crop from its farmers.

Fall was the shortest but most beautiful season when the cornfields turned brownish maize in color, the days grew shorter and crisper and the trees dazzled residents every year with color "even better than last year!" The brilliant crimsons, oranges, browns, yellows, greens and myriad other hues were breathtaking to behold. It was harvest time and the village was abuzz as the farmers brought in their crops for market.

But Ol' Man Winter was no stranger to Almont. Temperatures below freezing and lots of snow were common in most years. During the winter, the men repaired their machinery, tended to the livestock and made ready the seeds for planting in the spring. The women made baked goods and made or mended clothing along with dozens of other chores and wrote letters to their soldiers.

Almont continued to progress and the following humorous entry to the book *The History of Lapeer County, Michigan* appeared about the 1860 annual town meeting:

*"In the proceedings of the annual town meeting appears an evidence of the advance of civilization a resolution that hogs*

*be not allowed to run at large, and that the board provide a pound."* It does say hogs, not dogs.

By early 1861, however, the peaceful village was stirring as rumors of civil war circulated. There was no telegraph in Almont and no railroad line yet so reliable information had to come by stage coach or horseback. Mail came about once a week through Postmaster Daniel W. Richardson. Farmers and others made their way to Detroit, Port Huron or other places often enough that the village could have a good idea of what was happening in the Union. Michigan was a solidly Union state with Almont concurring.

Prior to the war Michigan was very active in the Underground Railroad, harboring fleeing slaves on their way to Canada. One safe house was in Utica about 20 miles south of Almont. Fugitive slaves were told to look for it 24 miles north of Detroit City Hall and twelve miles east of Pontiac Courthouse in Macomb County. The Lerich family, who owned the place, fed, clothed and housed the runaways in a log house. The family devised a fence for fugitives to slide down to the spring that emptied into the Clinton River, in order to more easily throw dogs off the slaves' tracks. The Lerichs also trafficked these fugitives to other locations on the Underground Railroad in the family wagon, hidden between bags of hay. Prior to the Civil War, the Lerichs had many visits from Sojourner Truth herself, as well as Frederick Douglas and Peter Jaxson. It is reasonable to believe that fleeing slaves passed through Almont on their way to other safe houses.

With the inauguration of Republican Abraham Lincoln as President on March 4, 1861, the war clouds gathered. In response to President Lincoln's orders, Michigan's new Governor, Austin Blair, called for troops over the next few years to put down the rebellion, preserve the Constitution and save the Union.

Almont responded and became a beehive of activity as the village set up an enlistment center. Under the state's Adjutant General, John R. Robertson, local officials were responsible for most of the recruiting of Civil War soldiers. Fifty-one year old farmer John B. Hough was elected Almont town supervisor in 1860 and held the post until after the war. He was named War Commissioner, for the duration of the war and was later a Probate Judge. D.E. Hazen was the village clerk throughout the war.

From 1861 to 1865 more than 250 men coming from the village and surrounding townships enlisted in Almont, serving in 16 different units. There were businessmen, professionals, farriers, musicians and others but most were farmers or farm laborers.

In the September 6, 1861 edition, the *Detroit Daily Advertiser* reported:

*"Our patriotic volunteers cannot feel neglected so long as the noble ladies of our State constantly evince their sympathy for them by furnishing everything possible conducive to their comfort. The ladies of Almont have forwarded fifty-one quilts to the company from that place now attached to Col. Broadhead's cavalry regiment (Company L of the 1st Michigan Cavalry). They resolved at a meeting held Wednesday, to furnish other articles necessary for the comfort of the company, as soon as possible."*

The military units Almont men served in were: (see appendix for names of all men) 1st Michigan Cavalry, 4th Michigan Cavalry, 5th Michigan Cavalry, 7th Michigan Cavalry, 8th Michigan Cavalry, 3rd Michigan Infantry, 5th Michigan Infantry, 10th Michigan Infantry, 15th Michigan Infantry, 16th Michigan Infantry (including sharpshooters unit), 22nd Michigan Infantry, 24th Michigan Infantry, 30th Michigan Infantry, 1st Michigan Engineers, 1st Michigan Colored Infantry and the 1st Michigan Light Artillery.

There were, of course, unspeakable atrocities committed by both sides and some Almont recruits, unfortunately, were deserters, dishonorably discharged or missing in action. But the vast majority served honorably, answering the call to duty to the fullest. Sixteen Almonters made the ultimate sacrifice from wounds sustained in the war with another nineteen dead of disease or other causes.

The civilians of Almont and Michigan were affected by the war also. In addition to having their loved ones in harm's way leaving fewer people to get the work done, inflation rose, credit was tighter and there was some concern that the war would not be confined to the South. Manufacturers began to make war material, farms provided foodstuffs and livestock for the military, community organizations and churches made blankets, socks and other items for the troops.

The waiting, the interminable waiting, for news of their men was the worst hardship of all.

The township and village were–and are–proud of their sons of the Civil War (many of whom are interred in national as well as local cemeteries) and the brave civilians who also did their part. Some of their descendants live in the Almont area still.

All, indeed, answered the call to duty.

# CHAPTER FOUR

# THE CIVIL WAR IN BRIEF

With billions of words having been written about the American Civil War, it is impossible in these few pages to cover every aspect and battle of the conflict. But we can offer a short summary to put into context the effort and sacrifice made by the military and civilian participants on both sides.

The feud between the North and the South had been festering since the Declaration of Independence was signed in 1776. There were huge differences in culture, style and economics, i.e. states' rights, agrarian vs. industrial society, tariffs, etc. But it was the South's "peculiar institution" of slavery begun in America in 1619 that made the pot boil over. The disputes over the expansion of the United States westward became primarily a question of admitting Free States or Slave States.

In January 1861, after the election of Republican Abraham Lincoln as President, an outspoken opponent of slavery, the South Carolina legislature voted to secede from the union. Mississippi, Florida, Alabama, Georgia, Louisiana and Texas followed forming the Confederate States of America.

Lincoln was inaugurated on March 4, 1861 and just five weeks later on, April 12th the South fired on Fort Sumter in Charleston Harbor starting the Civil War which would turn out to be the bloodiest war ever fought on American soil. Virginia, Arkansas, Tennessee and North Carolina joined the Confederacy after the firing on Fort Sumter. Part of Virginia did not want to secede so the state of West Virginia was formed and remained loyal to the union.

**President Lincoln's First Inauguration, U. S. Capitol, March 4, 1861 (National Archives)**

Confederate Vice President Alexander Stephens claimed that the "cornerstone" of the new government rested *"upon the great truth that the Negro is not equal to the white man; that slavery (or subordination to the superior race) is his natural and normal condition. This, our new government, is the first, in the history of the world, based upon this great physical, philosophical, and moral truth."*

Historian William J. Cooper Jr., in his book about Confederate President Jefferson Davis, said *"From at least the time of the American Revolution white southerners defined their liberty, in part, as the right to own slaves and to decide the fate of the institution without any outside interference."*

On April 15th, after the fall of Fort Sumter, President Lincoln issued a proclamation calling for the states to provide 75,000 troops to repulse the insurrection and reunite the Union. Michigan's quota was 780 officers and men. Governor Austin Blair responded immediately and more than the required men were enlisted in a fairly short time.

Organizing the 1st Michigan Infantry Regiment was completed on April 29th and it mustered into Federal service on May 1, 1861 with a total of 798 men. The President had called for a three month tour of duty, expecting that the rebellion could be quashed in that amount of time. The 1st left the state on May 13, 1861 and was the first regiment from a western state to reach Washington D.C., where it arrived on May 16th to guard the capital. When the 1st Michigan arrived in Washington, Lincoln is believed to have said, "Thank God for Michigan!"

Troops guard Washington from one of the many forts that surrounded the city.
(Brady photo, National Archives)

Instead of being over in three months, the first part of the war proved very grim for the Union. The Confederates defeated the North in two battles near Manassas, Virginia in 1862, Fredericksburg, Virginia at the end of that year, and numerous other battles and skirmishes with very heavy loss of life.

But on September 17, 1862, Confederate forces under General Robert E. Lee were caught by General McClellan near Sharpsburg, Maryland. This battle along the Antietam Creek proved to be the bloodiest day of the war; 2,108 Union soldiers were killed and 9,549 wounded and 2,700 Confederates were killed and 9,029 wounded.

The battle had no clear winner, but because General Lee withdrew to Virginia, McClellan was considered the victor. The battle convinced both the British and French, who were contemplating official recognition of the Confederacy, to reconsider and gave Lincoln the opportunity to announce his Emancipation Proclamation which would free all slaves in areas rebelling against the United States, effective January 1, 1863.

In the Western Theater the North beat the South at Shiloh in Hardin County, Tennessee. It was at this battle that General Ulysses S. Grant became well known.

Lincoln's generals never pressed their advantage thus prolonging the war. During the course of the war, Lincoln appointed Generals Irvin McDowell, George McClellan, John Pope, Ambrose Burnside, Joseph Hooker, George Meade, and Ulysses S. Grant to be Union Commanders. Grant would finally lead the Union to victory.

But it was Meade who turned the tide decisively for the North at the Battle of Gettysburg. Lee had moved north in order to gain a victory on Union soil and the two large armies met in July 1863 in the Pennsylvania village of Gettysburg. Gettysburg was a crossroads of 10 major routes. There would be a major advantage for whichever side controlled them.

For three days in the warm weather the great armies clashed. The battle evolved seeing both sides with a temporary advantage. The Union, however, held on and on the decisive third day, July 3rd, Lee launched what became known as "Pickett's Charge." It was 87 degrees and muggy at the time of this encounter. After Confederate attacks on both Union flanks had failed the day and night before, Lee was determined to strike the Union center on the third day. General Meade correctly anticipated this move and had his forces arranged accordingly.

**Fighting on both sides was furious. (National Archives)**

While this action was in progress, J. E. B. Stuart's cavalry tried to go around and attack the Union rear. The Michigan Brigade of the Union cavalry met the Confederates and successfully stopped the attack and made the rebels retreat.

**A cavalry charge at Gettysburg (National Archives)**

The infantry assault was preceded by a massive artillery bombardment that was meant to soften up the Union defense and silence its artillery, but it was largely ineffective with the ordnance falling harmlessly behind Union lines.

During "Pickett's Charge" led by General George E. Pickett's Division, approximately 12,500 Confederates in nine infantry brigades advanced over open fields for nearly a mile under heavy Union artillery and rifle fire. Although about 300 Confederates were able to breach the low stone wall that shielded many of the Union defenders, they could not maintain their hold and were repulsed with more than 50% casualties, a decisive defeat that ended the three-day battle and Lee's campaign into Pennsylvania and the North.

In the Western Theater the fall of Vicksburg, Mississippi on the next day, July 4th, meant that the Union gained complete control over the Mississippi River, cutting off the westernmost portions of the Confederacy. Though the South scored a major victory at Chickamauga in northwestern Georgia, by 1864 the tide was running with the North. Union victories at Chattanooga, and Franklin, Tennessee essentially destroyed the Confederate Army of Tennessee. The Union took Mobile, Alabama, the last major port on the Gulf Coast, and by the end of the year Atlanta had fallen to Union troops, paving the way for the March to the Sea by Gen. William Tecumseh Sherman's forces, which reached Savannah by the end of the year, devastating the Confederate heartland and cutting the eastern Confederacy in half. Grant and his generals

**Confederate General Robert E. Lee**
**(Brady photo, National Archives)**

kept pressing the attack against rebel forces and the attrition showed.

The Union took the Confederate capital, Richmond, Virginia, in April 1865. Historians generally regard the surrender of the Army of Northern Virginia by General Robert E. Lee to General Ulysses S. Grant, at the village of Appomattox Court House on April 9, 1865 as the end of the Confederate States and the war. Some Confederate arms and flags were presented to the 16th Michigan Infantry. The 4th Michigan Cavalry captured President Davis at Irwinville, Georgia on May 10th, and the remaining Confederate armies had surrendered by June 1865. After the assassination, the 24th Michigan Infantry, part of the famous Iron Brigade, escorted President Lincoln's body back Springfield, Illinois and guarded his tomb.

Michiganians and Almonters played important parts in nearly every encounter in the war.

There were several reasons for the terrible carnage of the war. Armies always seem to fight the last war. The generals had been taught the "Napoleonic" tactics where men in regiments moved and stood shoulder-to-shoulder facing the enemy. The first rank would fire their weapons and while they reloaded, the second rank would fire.

**The men stood shoulder-to-shoulder as in this reenactment (photo courtesy Ken Giorlando)**

In Napoleon's time they used smooth bore muskets firing a round lead ball. These guns were accurate to only 75 to 100 yards or so at best. So the object was to throw as much lead as possible at the enemy making it more likely to hit a man. These regiments could then charge the enemy because of the closer range and, hopefully, overrun them before they could reload.

But by the time of the Civil War, the armies used rifles. The barrels had a groove etched inside and a cone-shaped lead projectile to fire. These weapons were accurate at much greater distances – 200 to 300 yards up to 800 yards. Now men standing close together made easier targets while the opponents could stand farther apart. Thus, with accurate fire and a lead bullet nearly the size of a man's thumb (.58 caliber) the number of men killed or wounded rose dramatically.

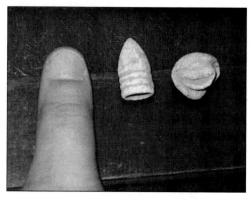

.58 caliber unfired and fired lead bullets found at Gettysburg (author photo)

Couple that with the fact that medical techniques were not very advanced, many of the wounded died of their wounds. This was because of less than sanitary conditions, no antibiotics, untrained medical personnel and an overwhelming number of casualties to treat.

Michigan Private Levi C. Clark wrote in his diary on September 4, 1864:

*"Sunday. Went to town to see the wounded rebels and our own wounded. A very affecting sight to see some with their legs off, others with their arms off. Some wounded in part and some another."*

Sometimes field surgeons on both sides could only amputate wounded limbs under no sanitary conditions. Some men reported how the amputated arms and legs "stacked up like cord wood."

More than 620,000 combatants died on both sides from wounds or disease, nearly 2% of the adult male population.

Every soldier was affected by the field conditions and experiences of war, yet they still answered the call to duty.

# CHAPTER FIVE

# TO BE A CIVIL WAR SOLDIER

When the men of Almont and other small towns enlisted in the army early in the war most of them had no idea what they were getting into. It was an adventure and chance to be away from home and the farm, maybe a chance to make some money. They were patriotic, enthusiastic even eager. Jason Clark, 10th Michigan Infantry, wrote:

> *"Let the traitors die but the union be preserved. May the stars and stripes never cease to float over the U.S. and I expect to be a soldier until the glorious banner does wave over every part of the land in the union or else find a soldier's grave in the land of war and strife amidst the roaring of cannon and the blasting of steel. And if that should be the case I shall die feeling that I have done what I could do to preserve the country that forefathers fought so hard for to gain."*

Most of the men thought that the war would be over in a very short time. Later in the war, however, after several Union defeats, it was obvious that the war would not be over quickly and men had second thoughts. A draft was instituted, bounties raised and other incentives instituted. A man could even buy a substitute for himself for $300. But most still enlisted of their own free will.

A few of them had probably ridden a horse. Many had probably fired a rifle at some potential food. Riding a horse swinging a sabre while the other rider was trying to kill you just wouldn't have been contemplated or practiced.

And firing a rifle at another man who was very much like you was a lot harder, physically and emotionally, than shooting a squirrel especially when the other guy had a rifle also and was trying to kill you. Few had ever done that before. The other guy was a young recruit too, scared and probably away from home for the first time. He probably had a family and was needed at home to work his farm or business just like the Almonter. But off to war they went.

At first, many of the men had no uniform and it would be a while before one army wore blue and the other grey. But soon they were issued two coats, one a frock coat considered the dress uniform and a sack coat, much like fatigues in which they would go into battle. These were accompanied by wool sky blue pants, suspenders and two shirts made of wool flannel. Most men discarded these uncomfortable shirts for cotton ones sent from home.

**Michigan troops sported state Coat of Arms buttons (author photo)**

A typical Union enlisted man's
uniform, Gettysburg National Park
(author photos)

Underwear and socks were more than likely provided by the men's families who usually kept a good supply coming from home.

Most of the men wore a slouch hat or "kepi" which was black, wide brimmed and looked a lot like a mini-stove pipe hat the was falling forward. There was also a similar forage cap with smaller tilt at the top.

Shoes were ankle height, made of leather and had heavy leather soles and heels. Many did not come in right or left foot. Only weeks of wear would make them match the respective foot. Some of the men put steel plates on the heels

to make them last longer. The soldiers sometimes marched up to 30 or 40 miles a day in these shoes.

After he was clothed, the soldier carried a muzzle loading rifle which was made of wood and steel, nearly five feet long (longer with the bayonet attached for close-in fighting) and weighing about nine pounds. Cavalrymen also carried pistols and a sabre.

A soldier wore a leather belt with a large, brass buckle to which he attached a scabbard for storing his bayonet and a small box carrying the brass caps which sparked when hit by the rifle's hammer igniting the gunpowder inside the barrel, thus firing the rifle.

A leather cartridge box carrying his lead bullets was slung over his shoulder. The bullets, about the size of a thimble, were attached to paper cartridges containing the right amount of black gunpowder. These were placed in the muzzle of the weapon and rammed "home" with a ramrod stored on the rifle.

All men carried a canteen for clean, fresh water which sometimes was in short supply. And each carried a black knapsack on his back that was made from tarred canvas to make it fairly rain resistant.

Men carried all sorts of personal items in this such as extra clothing, a water cup, a metal plate, rations, eating utensils, comb, toothbrush, soap, paper and pencil for writing letters to home, tobacco, a bible, playing cards, etc. Above the knapsack he carried a rolled up blanket. Most also carried a haversack over their shoulder, about a foot square with a water proof lining, that was used to carry more personal items, rations and maybe some snacks like apples.

All of this gear weighed forty to fifty pounds, about like carrying three to four bowling balls along. Sometimes the man would simply discard some of the equipment to have less weight to carry.

## CAMP LIFE

Being in battle is one of the most terrifying experiences a man can have. The "kill or be killed" axiom can sober up a man in a hurry and test his strength, courage, faith and myriad other emotions. As Union General William Tecumseh Sherman famously said, "War is hell."

But, thankfully, very little of a soldier's time was spent in combat. Much of his time was spent in camp or marching to another location.

A typical Union camp. Note the lack of trees. They were used for firewood, etc. (Brady photo, National Archives)

The camps could be very muddy after a rain and very dusty after a day of sunshine and the mosquitoes and other critters were in no short supply to annoy the troops.

Several men lived together in canvas tents in the camp. There were several designs of tents but all were hot in summer and cold in winter, especially when the ventilation flaps were closed to keep out the rain. Usually a treated canvas cloth or boards made the floor. It should be recalled that deodorant was non-existent and clean water for a bath was scarce so imagine the aroma in the tents. Add to this open latrines and horse manure and a civil war camp could be a rather unpleasant place to be.

Occasionally, if they had time, the men built small shanties from lumber and logs. These, of course, allowed the men a little more protection from the elements.

On December 23, 1864, Levi C. Clark, 10th Michigan Infantry wrote:

> *"Clear but very cold. Finished our shanty sides built of logs. Some boards to the bottom to lay on. 2 letters from home."*

The camps were usually set up in an orderly fashion with regiments grouped together and officers and men separated.

**Union soldiers in camp getting ready to march (Brady photo, National Archives)**

The average soldier's day began at about 5 or 6 a.m. with reveille and roll call. The men then had breakfast consisting of some corn bread and maybe some beans, salt pork, or bacon, if they were lucky. Hardtack was a ubiquitous staple, too. It is a simple type of cracker or biscuit made from flour, water, and sometimes salt. Inexpensive and long-lasting, it was used for sustenance in the absence of perishable foods. The men also drank coffee. Union men usually had an abundance of coffee, a luxury not shared by the Confederates. They crushed the coffee beans with a rock or gun butt and brewed up their liquid delight. It was used to soften the hardtack as well.

After breakfast, it was drill, drill, drill. These sessions lasted two hours or so and there were as many as five sessions a day. The men drilled on maneuvers and weapons use. Learning discipline and obeying orders were paramount requirements in the drills. This could be trying with recruits fresh from home.

Between drills the men cleaned up the camp, foraged for wood, water and food, built roads, dug latrines and otherwise tried to make camp life better. Some men were always on guard duty. Jason Clark, 10th Michigan Infantry, wrote in a letter to his sister:

*"We were out on a forageing [sic] expedition yesterday and didn't get in camp till [sic] 11 o'clock at night. I was tired, hungry and footsore and we expect to go on picket tomorrow. But a soldier's life is different than any other life. We can't tell one hour what orders we will get the next hour"*

**A sutler's row in Tennessee (Brady photo, National Archives)**

Clean fresh water was, of course, a necessity and sometimes hard to find. Many men suffered and died of disease because of a lack of clean water. Fresh vegetables were scarce also so many men suffered from scurvy.

In most camps one or more sutlers set up shop. The sutler was a merchant who offered many goods that were not standard issue such as tobacco, candy, newspapers, shoelaces, etc. Their prices were not cheap but the men could be desperate for these items and spent much of their pay with the sutler.

During down time, a soldier read, wrote letters home, played games, gambled, fought with each other, swore and made true the old saying "boys will be boys." Alcohol was forbidden but widespread anyway.

And, of course, there were the prostitutes. Thousands of them were there to comfort the troops. With no antibiotics, many men died of venereal disease although that was very seldom listed as the official cause of death.

Most of the rest of a man's time was spent marching either seeking or avoiding the enemy. Levi Clark wrote:

*"Nov. 30 (1864) Clear. Lay in camp all day. Could not move on account of the rebels. Had a skirmish with them."*
*"Jan. 20 (1865) Clowdy. [sic] Left Savannah this morning at 8 o'clock for someplace I know not where. Marched 10 miles bushwacked in fine woods. Pitched our tent. Rainy after noon. Went to bed wet."*

On February 12, 1865 he wrote:

*"Sunday. Warm train guards again. Crossed the Charleston and Augusta Railroad at a little town called Willeston. Marched 16 miles. Our company detailed on guard. I had to stand 2 hours."*

A soldier's life was anything but glamorous but most still answered the call to duty.

# CHAPTER SIX

**The Soldiers Stories**

**Norvell F. Churchill, Farmer, 1st Michigan Cavalry**

I often wonder how history might have been different if this event had happened or that had not happened. What if Hitler had stuck with painting or John Wilkes Booth to acting? What if Lee Harvey Oswald had missed? What would have happened if there had been no George Washington, John Adams or Thomas Jefferson? Would someone other than Henry Ford have put the world on wheels? If Lincoln had found someone like Grant earlier, would the Civil War have been over much earlier? What if Custer had died long before the Battle of the Little Bighorn? All interesting things to ponder, and certainly history would have unfolded differently, but we'll never know "what if...."

The flamboyant Gen. Custer in one of his custom-made uniforms (Brady photo, National Archives)

George Armstrong Custer grew up in Monroe, Michigan living with his half sister and her husband and graduated from West Point last in his class of 34 in 1861. At the outset of the Civil War he was assigned to the cavalry.

His first action was at the first battle of Bull Run (Manassas) where he was mostly a messenger and staff officer with little battle experience. But he did woo his superiors and just before the Battle of Gettysburg in 1863, the 5' 11" Custer was promoted from Captain to Brigadier General, the youngest at 23, and given command of the Michigan Cavalry Brigade consisting of the 1st, 5th, 6th and 7th Michigan Cavalry regiments. He was so green, he had to earn the respect of his troops but that he did with his flamboyance and daring.

He wore a hand-made uniform of flannel and velvet with gold braiding and buttons as well as a bright red scarf around his neck that some of his troops adopted as a trademark. He certainly had a flair for the dramatic and his own self promotion.

Norvell (sometimes spelled Norville or Norval) Francis Churchill was born on June 11, 1840 and raised on a farm in Berlin Township, just east of Almont, Michigan. When the Civil War broke out, Churchill answered President Lincoln's and Governor Blair's call for volunteers and on August 14, 1861, he enlisted in Almont for three years of service and was assigned to Company L of the 1st Michigan Cavalry Regiment formed by Almonter Capt. Melvin Brewer and left for service in September.

Norvell's brothers also became soldiers. Peter, the oldest, served in the 5th

**Private Norvell Churchill**
**(Courtesy Richard J. Webb, Churchill's great-grandson)**

Michigan Infantry as did Judson. Nelson was in the 5th Michigan Cavalry.

Assigned mostly guard duty, the 1st was in combat with the Confederates at Orange Court House, Virginia, July 16th., then at Cedar Mountain, Virginia, on August 9th, where an engagement took place between Union Major General Nathaniel P. Bank's force and the superior forces of Rebels Thomas J. "Stonewall" Jackson, Gen. Robert S. Ewell and Lieutenant General Ambrose Powell Hill, with the 1st suffering heavy casualties.

Moving to Centerville, Virginia, the regiment was engaged at the second Battle at Manassas, or Bull Run, on the 30th of August, resulting in 7 men killed, 13 wounded, 7 captured with 106 missing. The unit's commander, Colonel Thornton Broadhead, was among the mortally wounded.

During the early part of 1863, the regiment was engaged in guard duty in front of the defenses of Washington where duty was arduous and as difficult as the regiment had ever been ordered to perform. The 1st lost thirty men during this period to repeated attacks by Mosby's Guerrillas.

In June the regiment set out in pursuit of Lee's forces, then moving north into Maryland and Pennsylvania. When the Union command was re-organized near the end of June 1863, the regiment was re-assigned to the Michigan Brigade, under the command of Custer.

A battle ensued at Hanover on June 30th, just outside of Gettysburg and on July 2, 1863 General George Meade, Union commander at Gettysburg, posted the cavalry to protect the army's flank. To the north, near the village of Hunterstown, Custer and the Michigan Brigade collided with Confederate General Wade Hampton's troops on the Hunterstown Road. After posting concealed skirmishers from the 6th and 7th Michigan Cavalry Regiments along both sides of the road, Custer led a charge with about 60 men down the center of the narrow, fence lined road directly toward the Southerners. Custer's plan was to attack and then retreat hoping to lure the Southerners into chasing him into a trap with his concealed men. But during the charge, fierce fighting ensued with men from both cavalry units firing their weapons. In the first volley Custer's horse went down, shot from under him, leaving him on foot surrounded by rebel troops all trying to kill him. Custer fought bravely but was hopelessly outnumbered and had no way to escape.

Young Private Norvell Churchill of the 1st Michigan Cavalry, seeing Custer in desperate straits, spurred his mount and dashed through the Confederates to Custer's side. Churchill fended off several rebels with his sabre and reportedly shot one of those closest to Custer. Then he reached down, and taking Custer's hand, swung the young General up on his horse behind him and they raced together to safety. Custer had been saved. Both lived to fight another day. Churchill became one of Custer's trusted orderlies and served with distinction for the rest of the war.

In his rather un-detailed official report Custer failed to mention this significant event. He wrote:

*"On July 2, at the battle of Hunterstown, one squadron, under command of Captain Duggan, was detailed to hold the road leading into the town from the right front of it. One platoon was deployed as skirmishers on the left of the road leading into town from the rear. This platoon was actively engaged and did good service."*

The Michigan Brigade was in another fierce battle at Gettysburg on the next day, July 3rd as they intercepted J.E.B. Stuart's cavalry attempting to circle behind Union lines while "Pickett's Charge" was taking place to the Union front. Confederate commander General Robert E. Lee's strategy was to cut the Union forces in half. It can be argued that Custer's action as he shouted "Come on, you Wolverines!" and led his men on a full-gallop charge driving Stuart's men back turned the tide of battle, and the war, to the Union.

In this official report on this action, Custer singled out Private Churchill, one of the few enlisted men cited, for special praise.

*"I desire to commend to your favorable notice…Orderlies Norval [sic] Churchill, company L, First Michigan cavalry,*

*George L. Foster, company C, First Michigan cavalry, and Benjamin H. Butler, company M, First Michigan cavalry."*

Following Gettysburg, the brigade served with great honor for the rest of the war, engaging in many more battles including, the Wilderness, Cold Harbor, Winchester and was there at Appomattox Court House for the surrender of General Robert E. Lee.

**Norvell, Hannah and family on the farm**
**(Courtesy Richard J. Webb)**

Private Churchill was honorably discharged on February 25, 1865 and he moved back to Michigan. Custer visited him on his farm near Romeo and tried to talk him into joining the western campaign. Churchill politely, but wisely, declined.

Norvell married Hannah Savage on December 30, 1874. They had eight children. In 1878, the Churchills moved to a farm in Echo, Antrim County, Michigan, where he raised cattle, swine, cash crops and lumber. Many of his descendents still live in the area.

He died on June 25, 1905 and was laid to rest in Dinsmore Cemetery, Echo Township.

History might have turned out very differently without the heroics of Almont's own Norvell F. Churchill who answered the call to duty.

On July 2, 2008 a monument was dedicated in Hunterstown, Pennsylvania commemorating the event.

**This monument stands today in Hunterstown**
**(author photo)**

**Lt. Col. Melvin Brewer, Almonter**
**Formed and led Company L, 1st Michigan Cavalry**
**One of those who answered the call to duty**
**(Michigan State Archives)**

## Lieut. Col. Melvin Brewer, Attorney, 1st Michigan Cavalry

On April 15, 1861, President Abraham Lincoln issued a proclamation calling for the states to raise 75,000 troops to defend the Union. In part, he said:

> *"I appeal to all citizens to favor, facilitate, and aid in this effort to maintain the honor, the integrity, and the existence of our National Union, and the perpetuity of popular government, and to redress wrongs already long enough endured."*

Eleven days later, Attorney Melvin Brewer wrote the following letter offering to organize a company for the Union Army:

**Michigan State Archives**

Brewer then recruited and led Company L of the 1st Michigan Calvalry. After training, guarding Washington was the first responsibility of the regiment. In early 1863, battles in Virginia at Winchester, Harrisonburg, Middletown, Orange Court House, Strasburg, Second Bull Run, Greenwich, Thorofare Gap and Cedar Mountain tested the unit's mettle. It tested positive.

In late June, the regiment was assigned to the Michigan Cavalry Brigade along with the 5th, 6th and 7th Michigan Cavalry Regiments under the command of newly appointed 23 year-old Brigadier General George Armstrong Custer, who would attain immortality later.

And then came the Battle of Gettysburg. The little village of Gettysburg and the surrounding area became the site of the most renowned battle of the war. This Union victory, under General George Meade, was the "high water mark" of the Confederacy.

According to Don Harvey in www.michiganinthewar.org:

*"Under its new organization, now consisting of the 1st., Colonel Town, the 5th., Colonel Alger, the 6th., Colonel Gray and the 7th., Colonel Mann all under the command of Brigadier General Custer the reunited Brigade prepared to enter upon the great battle of Gettysburg."*

It should be noted that throughout his service with the cavalry, now promoted Major Brewer furnished his own horses and equipment rather than rely on government issued animals.

On June 30, 1863 they were heavily engaged at Hanover, then on the 1st of July marched toward York, passing through Abbotsville to Berlin, encamping there that night. The next day they were engaged at Hunterstown where Almonter Norvell Churchill saved Custer from being killed followed on July 3rd with a pivotal engagement east of Gettysburg.

In the advance, and the early engagements with the Confederates, then throughout the whole battle as well as in the pursuit of the retreating southerners, the brigade took a prominent part, distinguishing itself for bravery and achievement in every encounter, finally making a most gallant attack on the Confederate rear guard at Falling Waters, driving them to the river, killing many and capturing large numbers.

The action of July 3rd, with the 1st Michigan Cavalry, part of the Michigan Brigade with its contingent of Almonters under Brewer, played a key role with a mounted charge so bold it is talked of still.

It is said that Custer never sent men into battle, he led them. Outnumbered 10 to 1, Custer galloped ahead of his troops, sabre in hand, (see cover) with his men yelling and fighting furiously hand-to-hand thus halting Gen. J.E.B. Stuart's effort to get behind Union lines about eight miles east of Gettysburg. This was vital in the Union victory and turning the tide in the war. Had Stuart's men gone around the Union's rear, the battle, and history, may have turned out very differently.

A total of nearly 4,000 Michiganians fought at Gettysburg, with more than 1,100 of them becoming casualties. The 1st lost six officers and eighty men."

Here is what General Custer said in his official report:

*"Arriving within a few yards of the enemy's column, the charge was ordered, and with a yell that spread terror before them, the First Michigan cavalry, led by Colonel Town, rode upon the front rank of the enemy, and sabring all who came within reach. For a moment, but only a moment, that long, heavy column stood its ground; then, unable to withstand the impetuosity of our attack, it gave way in a disorderly rout, leaving cast numbers of dead and wounded in our possession, while the First, being masters of the field, had the proud satisfaction of seeing the much-vaunted chivalry, led by their favorite commander, seek safety in headlong flight. I cannot find language to express my high appreciation of the gallantry and daring displayed by the officers and men of the First Michigan cavalry. They advanced to the charge of a vastly superior force with as much order and precision as if going upon parade; and I challenge the annals of warfare to produce a more brilliant or successful charge of cavalry than the one just recounted."*

But Gettysburg was hardly the end of the war for the Michigan Cavalry Brigade. Far from it. The brigade was also strategically engaged in the following battles.

In Maryland, Monterey, Smithtown, Boonesborough, Hagerstown, Williamsport, Falling Waters. In Virginia, Kelly's Ford, Culpepper Court, White's Ford, James City, Brandy Station, Stevensburg, Morton's Ford, Richmond, Wilderness, Beaver Dam Station, Yellow Tavern, Cold Harbor, Leetown, Travillion Station, Winchester, Front Royal, Sheperdstown, Berryville, Summit, Opequan, Luray, Madison Court House, Louisa Court House, Five Forks, South Side Railroad, Sayler's Creek, Appomattox Court House and many more battles and skirmishes.

Throughout the war the Michigan Brigade suffered nearly 21% casualties, with 265 killed in action, 120 dying of their wounds and 880 dying of disease.

In June 1864, Major Melvin Brewer was commissioned as Lt. Col. having transferred to the 7th Michigan Cavalry. General Custer wrote the following to the Adjutant General of Michigan on July 3, 1864.

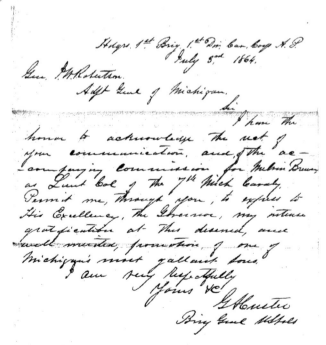

Now under overall command of General Philip Sheridan, but still led by Custer, raids in Virginia commenced on the 10th of May 1864. Trevilion Station, the largest all-cavalry battle of the war, was fought on June 11th and 12th. On June 11, Major Brewer was severely wounded in the left arm and sent for treatment to Seminary Hospital in Washington.

He was back on duty in early July and on the 31st the Brigade was ordered to proceed via Washington to the Shenandoah Valley in Virginia where they engaged the Confederates in hard fought battles at Winchester on August 11th, Front Royal on the 16th, Leetown the 25th, Sheperdstown the same day, then Smithfield on the 29th, Berryville, September 3rd and Summit the 4th, followed at Winchester on the 19th where the decisive battle was waged that essentially eliminated the Confederate Cavalry force as an effective fighting unit.

Three flags were captured but it was here, while advancing on horseback toward a stone house in Winchester occupied by unseen rebels, that Melvin Brewer was shot. He died on September 25, 1864.

Custer wrote:

*"He fell farthest in advance of those that on that day surrendered their lives in their country's cause. Possessed of ability qualifying him for much higher positions than those he filled, he was invariably selected to command expeditions involving danger and requiring experience, daring and sagacity. Known and respected by all his brother officers, his memory will always be cherished by every member of his command."*

And so, Almont's Melvin Brewer, who said he was "not very well informed in relation to military affairs" at the beginning, became an excellent cavalry officer and a true military hero defending the Union after his call to duty.

## Pvt. Charles H. Sitts, Farmhand, 1st Michigan Cavalry

When Civil War came to America in 1861, Charles H. Sitts was a farmhand near Almont, son of Jacob and Peggy Ann Sitts. He was 18 years old and good on a horse. Like most young men of the time, Charles wanted to serve his country and help preserve the Union, but he was also looking for a little adventure away from the farm. So he joined Company L of the 1st Michigan Cavalry Regiment, organized by Almonter Melvin Brewer from August 21 to September 6, 1861.

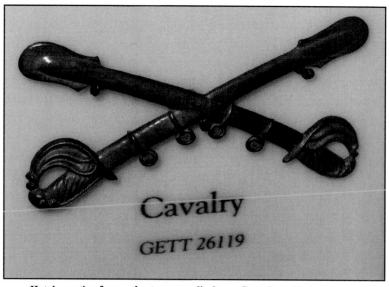

**Hat decoration for cavalry troops on display at Gettysburg National Park**
**(author photo)**

The regiment of 1,144 officers and men in 12 companies, including 39 Almonters, was mustered into Federal service on September 13th in Detroit and shipped out to Washington on the 29th under the command of Col. Thornton Broadhead.

Union cavalry units like the 1st Michigan had the following primary missions:

1. Reconnaissance and counter-reconnaissance screening
2. Defensive, delaying actions
3. Pursuit and harassment of defeated enemy forces
4. Offensive actions
5. Long-distance raiding against enemy lines of communications, supply depots, railroads, etc.

It was number three above that Pvt. Sitts was engaged in on July 4, 1863.

The 1st trained in cavalry tactics, though not nearly enough. They continued "on the job training" for the rest of the war. Occasionally, a cavalry unit would mount a full charge on horseback but most of the time the men fought while dismounted along skirmish lines. They usually worked in groups of four. Three would fight while one stood back out of range and held the horses.

After guard duty around Washington, the 1st moved under General Nathaniel Banks into Virginia headed to Winchester and the Shenandoah Valley. They were intercepted and thrown back by Confederates commanded by Thomas "Stonewall" Jackson.

They then moved to Orange Court House, Virginia in July and Cedar Mountain in August where they suffered heavy losses.

On August 30, 1862, the unit was engaged at the second Battle of Bull Run (Manassas) losing seven men killed, 13 wounded and 106 missing. Col. Broadhead was mortally wounded and died on September 5th. The 1st then went back to guarding Washington.

They set out for Maryland and Pennsylvania and in June 1863 as part of the Michigan Cavalry Brigade under the command of young Michigan Brigadier General George Armstrong Custer.

By all accounts, Private Sitts and his comrades fought furiously and well during the engagements. Custer himself reported that *"Nobly did the old First do its duty."*

The Battle of Gettysburg was fought over July 1st, 2nd, 3rd, a decisive victory for the North and Private Sitts and his comrades played a significant part in it.

The following day, a rainy July [4th], the nation's birthday, as Lee retreated, segments of the Michigan Brigade were sent to intercept and disrupt his supply lines at Fairfield Gap. The following is from Gen. Custer's report of the action:

*"On July 4, the regiment moved with the division toward Monterey Gap. At Fountain Dale, was sent upon a road leading from the right of the town to Fairfield Gap, where the enemy was found occupying it. A charge was made by one squadron, under command of Lieutenant Colonel Stagg, with success and against superior numbers. The enemy was driven out and the Gap held until the entire column and train had passed. Here the regiment sustained a heavy loss. Colonel Stagg, in leading the charge, had his horse killed, and was himself seriously injured by the falling off the same. Here Capt. William R. Elliott was mortally wounded, and Lieut. James S. McElhenny killed; 17 men also lost. At Monterey Pass, the regiment lost 2 officers and 6 men."*

Private Sitts was one of the 17. He was dismounted in a skirmish position when a Confederate bullet found its mark.

Today Private Sitts, along with Almonter Pvt. Philip Wilcox Jr. of the same unit rests in peace in Gettysburg National Cemetery, in a united country, only a few yards from where President Lincoln uttered the "few appropriate remarks" known as the Gettysburg Address saying that "we here highly resolve that these dead shall not have died in vain." Indeed, they did not. They answered the call to duty.

**Private Sitts' gravestone at Gettysburg, spelled wrong.**
**(author photo)**

The New York Times reported on the Gettysburg Address this way:

*PRESIDENT LINCOLN'S ADDRESS.*

*The President then delivered the following dedicatory speech:*
*Fourscore and seven years ago our Fathers brought forth upon this Continent a new nation, conceived in liberty and dedicated to the proposition that all men are created equal. [Applause.] Now we are engaged in a great civil war, testing whether that nation, or any nation so conceived and so dedicated, can long endure. We are met on a great battle-field of that war. We have come to dedicate a portion of it as a final resting place of those who here gave their lives that that nation might live. It is altogether fitting and proper that we should do this. But in a larger sense, We cannot dedicate, We cannot consecrate, We cannot hallow this ground. The brave men, living and dead, who struggled here have consecrated it far above our power to add or detract. [Applause.] The world will little note nor long remember what we say here, but it can never forget what they did here. [Applause.] It is for us, the living, rather, to be dedicated to the unfinished work that those who suffered here have thus far so nobly carried on. [Applause.] It is rather for us to be dedicated to the great task remaining before us, that from these honored dead we take increased devotion to the cause for which they gave the last full measure of devotion; that we here highly resolve that the dead shall not have died in vain; [applause] that the Nation shall under God have a new birth of freedom, and that Governments of the people, by the people and for the people shall not perish from the earth. [Long continued applause.]*
*Three cheers were then given for the President and for the Governors of the States.*
*After the delivery of the addresses, the dirge and the benediction closed the exercises and the immense assemblage separated at about 4 o'clock.*

**President Lincoln (hatless, at left, looking down) at the ceremony at Gettysburg, Nov. 19, 1863 (Brady photo, National Archives)**

## Pvt. Benjamin F. Johnston, Teacher, 5th Michigan Cavalry

Andersonville. The mere mention of the word will send shivers up the spine of Civil War enthusiasts. A total of 12,913 Union soldiers died from malnutrition, disease, starvation and other inhuman reasons in Anderson Prison (Camp Sumter) in Georgia, the largest Southern prison camp of the war.

Upon arriving, one soldier said:

*"As we entered the place, a spectacle met our eyes that almost froze our blood with horror, and made our hearts fail within us. Before us were forms that had once been active and erect;—stalwart men, now nothing but mere walking skeletons, covered with filth and vermin. Many of our men, in the heat and intensity of their feeling, exclaimed with earnestness. 'Can this be hell?'"*

Almonter Pvt. Benjamin F. Johnston, 5th Michigan Cavalry, survived Andersonville. He was 33 years old and a teacher when he enlisted. Almonters Pvt. Andrew Hogan and Pvt. Perry McConnell, unfortunately, did not survive Andersonville.

Johnston enlisted in the 5th with Company A at Almont on August 16, 1862. The 5th was part of the famous Michigan Brigade consisting of the 1st, 5th, 6th and 7th Cavalry under the command of Gen. George Armstrong Custer. The Brigade fought mightily in the Battle of Gettysburg securing a Union victory and then continued to fight in Virginia against the troops of Fitzhugh Lee.

Taking overall command of the Union forces, Gen. Philip Sheridan launched a raid on May 10, 1864. On June 11th and 12th the unit fought the battle of Trevilian Station. The two-day battle resulted in 1,007 Union casualties, 102 killed in action, 470 wounded (including Almont's Maj. Melvin Brewer) and 435 missing or captured.

**Prison at Andersonville, Georgia. Many Union men did not survive here.**
**(Brady Photo, National Archives)**

Pvt. Johnston was one of 435 taken prisoner on June 11th. He was sent to Libby Prison in Richmond and from there to Andersonville.

Conditions at Andersonville were so terrible that on July 9, 1864, Sgt. David Kennedy of the 9th Ohio Cavalry wrote in his diary:

*"Wuld that I was an artist & had the material to paint this camp & all its horors or the tounge of some eloquent Statesman and had the privleage of expresing my mind to our hon. rulers at Washington, I should gloery to describe this hell on earth where it takes 7 of its ocupiants to make a shadow."* (Original spelling)

But Johnston defied the odds and survived. He was there until paroled March 25, 1865. More danger awaited him though.

Near the end of April, Johnston boarded the river steamer "Sultana" with hundreds of other returning Union troops for the trip north. Lee had surrendered to Grant on April 9th essentially ending the war. In Johnston's own words:

*" I was paroled out and sent to Vicksburg, Miss., arriving at Black River on the 1st of April 1865, crossed the river and went into camp, remaining there until the 24th of April, afterwards marching about four miles to Vicksburg where we went on board the steamer "Sultana."*

*My company being near the rear of the column would naturally fall on the lower deck and on the bow of the boat. We arrived at Memphis, Tenn., on the evening of the 28th of April, and the steamer stopped and unloaded three hundred hogsheads of sugar which detained her until nearly eleven o'clock at night. Left there about that hour and went up the river about four miles, where we stopped and took on a supply of coal to last as far as Cairo, Ill., leaving the barges about two o'clock in the morning of the 27th, when, after steaming up the river three more miles, the explosion took place.*

*Taking in the whole situation at a glance I got up, put on my shoes and waited for a favorable opportunity to leave the boat, realizing that I was safe on the boat as long as the fire did not affect me. When the opportunity presented itself I took off my blouse, hat and shoes, keeping on all my underclothing, and took an ambrotype likeness of my wife and boy, out of my blouse pocket and put it in my pants pocket so that if I was lost and ever found it would be the means of identifying me. I then put my left hand on the railing of the boat and jumped into the river and commenced swimming for the shore. After being in the water a short time a piece of board, about six inches wide and from six to seven feet long, came floating along in front of me. Having secured it and placed it under my breast I had no trouble in reaching an island, but on account of high water it was overflown.*

*After a great amount of trouble I finally succeeded in getting out of the river into the fork of a small tree and remained there until eight o'clock, when I was picked up by a steamer and taken to the Soldiers Home at Memphis. Left there the second day for Michigan."*

Johnston was very involved in Almont community service for the rest of his life. He opened a furniture store and was active in Congregational Church affairs, the Masons and other organizations. He also served as village president, trustee on the school board and Justice of the Peace. He died on March 1, 1914 in Almont. He, along with wife Betsey Ann, are interred in the Hough Cemetery.

The following poem was written by Pvt. Johnston while confined in Andersonville Prison after answering the call to duty.

# Prisoner's Appeal

Friends of Freedom, one and all,
Pray do listen when we call,
For release from this earthly hell,
The horrors which no tongue can tell,
Exposed we are to disease and death,
Lying upon the filthy earth,
Unprotected from storms and heat,
Little, unwholesome, food to eat.

Thirty-five thousand are here confined,
Inside these walls of Georgia Pine.
The acreage which we occupy,
Is twenty-two, both marsh and dry;
Completely covered over with filth,
Throwing off a sickening stench.
The only water to quench our thirst
Runs between the rebel's post.

Thousands confined in this stockade,
Volunteered their country's aid;
Left their homes and kindred too,
Protecting the flag, red, white and blue.
Many times we all have faced,
The cannon's mouth without disgrace,
Proving our willingness to fight,
Against oppression for freedom rights.

Through misfortune, not for crime,
We are in these walls confined,
Far away from home and friends,
Expecting soon our days to end;
Starving, thirsting every day,
Until our flesh has shank away,
Leaving nothing but skeletons,
For myriads of vermin to feast upon.

The sufferings here can ne'er be told,
By finite tongues, young or old;
Possessing one like Demosthenes,
Cannot describe the horrid scenes.
Neither the eloquence of Cicero,
Can proclaim them so you know,
Our true condition, our wretched state,
Language is wholly inadequate.

We love our homes and kindred too;
Must we here bid them adieu?
Remained confined inside this pen,
Until our days on earth do end,
Where no relief does ever come.
To the sick and fevered one,
No heart to sigh, no tear to shed,
O'er the dying and the dead.

Thirteen thousand heroic men,
Already have died inside this pen;
Died alone in deep distress,
Without a place for their head to rest,
Excepting upon the filthy ground,
Where lice and vermin can be found,

Completely covering their ghostly forms,
Before their spirit had fled and gone.

Again to our friends we do appeal,
To get us away before you yield,
For life's sake do all in your power.
We're growing weaker every hour,
Then, oh then, release us soon,
Or awe shall face that awful doom,
Dying alone without a friend,
Inside this filthy horrid pen.

## Philip Wilcox, Jr., Farmer, 1st Michigan Cavalry, Company L

Not much is known about Philip Wilcox, Jr. other than he was born in 1839, the ninth of thirteen children to Philip D. Wilcox and Tabitha Sterling Wilcox. The Wilcox family had moved to a farm near Almont from Rhode Island. Young Philip worked the farm with his father and siblings.

Love found the young Wilcox and he married his sweetheart, Mary Jane Foster, on Valentines Day, February 14, 1859 in Imlay Township. No children were born to the couple.

As with so many other young men at the time, the nation beckoned him. Captain Melvin Brewer recruited 20 year-old Wilcox who joined Brewer's Company L of the 1st Michigan Cavalry on August 14, 1861 as a Private. The unit mustered in Detroit on September 6th and marched off to war after training for a short time.

As mentioned earlier, the 1st participated in numerous actions of the war as part of Custer's Michigan Brigade.

The 1st saw action at Hunterstown on July 2, 1863 and July 3rd, the third day of the momentous and historic battle, a fierce but decisive engagement occurred a few miles east of Gettysburg on what is now known as East Cavalry Field.

As we know, fierce fighting occurred near Rummel's Farm when the two cavalry armies met. Custer ordered and led a high-speed, mounted charge directly at Stuart with the 7th Michigan staggering Stuart's forces.

Stuart tried again for a breakthrough by sending in the bulk of Wade Hampton's brigade, accelerating in formation from a walk to a gallop, sabres flashing, calling forth "murmurs of admiration" from their Union targets. Union horse artillery batteries attempted to block the advance with shell and canister, but the Confederates moved too quickly and were able to fill in for lost men, maintaining their momentum. Custer and Col. Charles H. Town led the 1st Michigan Cavalry into the fray at a gallop. A trooper from one of the Pennsylvania regiments observed:

*"As the two columns approached each other the pace of each increased, when suddenly a crash, like the falling of timber, betokened the crisis. So sudden and violent was the collision that many of the horses were turned end over end and crushed their riders beneath them."*

**Rummel's Farm and East Cavalry Field today. It was here that Custer led his Wolverines in a furious charge and Pvt. Wilcox gave his life. (author photo)**

But Custer and the Michiganians held their ground as Stuart and Gen. Wade Hampton retreated.

Two hundred nineteen men of Custer's Brigade were killed in action that day. One of them was Almont's Pvt. Philip Wilcox, Jr.

Gettysburg was a Union victory and Lee retreated into Virginia. From then on he was forced to fight mostly defensive engagements because of his losses.

Casualties for the three-day battle were 23,055 with 3,150 killed in action for the North and 23,231 for the Confederates of which 4,708 were killed.

Later that year on November 19th, President Lincoln helped dedicate the national cemetery in Gettysburg. Today Private Philip Wilcox Jr. lies very close to Almont Private Charles H. Sitts in honored repose in that cemetery. Both Almonters had answered the call to duty.

**Private Wilcox rests in Gettysburg National Cemetery. (author photo)**

## Addison R. Stone M.D., Doctor, 5<sup>th</sup> Michigan Cavalry

Civil War medical treatment left a lot to be desired. It is estimated that more than 250,000 Union men and 164,000 Confederates died of disease. When the war started, the Union Army medical corps numbered 87 men. By the end of the war there were more than 11,000. Most of those were contract, un-commissioned assistant surgeons. Almonter Dr. Addison R. Stone was one of them.

Dr. Stone and others would find conditions around a Union camp or battlefield less than ideal to say the least. The water was bad, open latrines were everywhere, there were maggots and mosquitoes by the millions. Personal hygiene was not well practiced. Men went days or even weeks between baths and "clean" clothes, usually washed in the nearest river.

Using the medical practice of the time, germs of blood poisoning, gangrene and lockjaw were, unfortunately, not uncommon. Surgeons would also undertake the most severe operations at the front, often under fire, under conditions in which even a pretense of surgical cleanliness could not have been maintained, even if the knowledge of the time had been sufficient to even try.

The men's diets were high in calories and low on vitamins. Seldom did the troops have fresh fruit and vegetables. They ate beef when available, salt pork, navy beans and hardtack, a biscuit that was usually stale. Many times the food was undercooked and usually fried.

Long lines of troops soon began to come to sick call complaining of loose bowels and various other internal problems. Tuberculosis, malaria, typhoid, blood poisoning and fever were also major worries. Some of these ailments plagued the men for the rest of their lives.

The assistant surgeon was in charge of deciding who got treated first and who could or could not return to duty, who should be hospitalized, etc. Being hospitalized was not a pleasant experience. Early in the war, the hospital was usually a large tent. Later, the army secured barns, farm houses and other buildings to serve as hospitals.

During a battle, the assistant surgeon would attempt to establish a dressing station as close to the front as possible. He and his men took as many instruments, bandages, opium pills, morphine, as well as bottles of brandy and whiskey as they could. Some wounded men walked in but most were brought in by stretcher. Those who had suffered head wounds, neck wounds or were "gut shot" were set aside because the wounds were probably mortal.

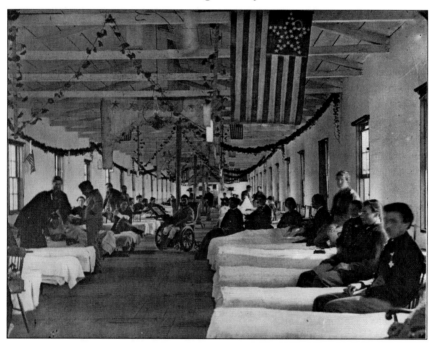

A Union hospital in Washington, D.C. (Brady photo, National Archives)

For the others, usually the victim was given a stiff drink to help diminish shock. The doctor then cleaned up the wound as best he could, removed bullets, usually by hand, and bandaged the man up to be sent back to the field hospital.

A majority of the wounds were in the arms and/or legs. Amputation was the most common treatment. It was not an easy operation under the dreadful conditions. Instruments were washed off in cold, bloody water. If an instrument was dropped it was picked up and continued being used. The wound was bandaged and the patient was given frequent doses of whiskey or quinine to calm them and ease the pain. The area around the doctors was littered with amputated arms and legs. The stench was horrendous. But amputations and the other medical procedures, however primitive, did save lives. Medicine, medical instruments and procedures advanced steadily during the war as the doctors learned more and more.

Dr. Stone enlisted at Almont in September 25, 1862 in the 5th Michigan Cavalry and served under Dr. John P. Wilson, surgeon. Stone was 34 when he enlisted, stood 5' 10 ½" tall, which was quite tall for the 1860s. He had married Ellen F. Jenness on May 7, 1857 in Detroit.

The 5th served as part of the defenses of the capital, Washington, shortly after Stone joined the Unit until June 1863. Over the next month the 5th, as part of the Michigan Brigade, took part in several major battles, including the Battle of Hanover on June 30, the Battle of Gettysburg from July 1st to July 3rd, and the Battle of Williamsport from July 6th to July 14th.

By September, Dr. Stone was becoming incapacitated, in his own words:

> "...on account of typhoid, pneumonia, general debility and a general breaking. Also complications of the heart which was caused by the exposure and hardships incident to the Gettysburg campaign."

He also had severe lung problems. In short, he was worse off than many of his patients.

After the Battle of Gettysburg, Stone was admitted to Officers Hospital in Georgetown (Washington, D.C.) where he was treated for several weeks. He was honorably discharged in September 1863 because of disability.

The doctor moved back to Almont and suffered ongoing symptoms of these maladies for the rest of his life. He did, however, open a medical practice in Almont across the street from Ben Johnston's furniture store.

He passed away on February 11, 1888 in Almont. He was joined in death by his wife, Ellen, on June 12, 1900. They both are now interred together in Hough Cemetery, Almont.

Dr. Stone had answered the call to duty.

**Dr. Stone's grave, Hough Cemetery, Almont (author photo)**

# The Roberts Brothers
## Sgt. Ephriam Roberts, Farmhand, 5<sup>th</sup> Michigan Cavalry
## Lt. Ami M. Roberts, Musician, 10<sup>th</sup> Michigan Infantry

Ephriam Roberts, was four years younger than Almont brother Ami. Ephriam had moved to Memphis, Michigan and enlisted in the 5th Michigan Cavalry, part of the Michigan Brigade under George Armstrong Custer, as a sergeant on August 14, 1862 at Riley, Michigan.

In addition to helping in the Union victory at Gettysburg by stopping J.E.B. Stuart's Confederate cavalry, the 5th fought many smaller skirmishes for the rest of 1863. In 1864 came the Battle of Morton's Ford on February 6th and 7th, and three months later the Overland Campaign began. The 5th Cavalry saw action in several battles of this campaign, including the Battle of the Wilderness near Fredericksburg, Virginia on May 6th and 7th and the Battle of Cold Harbor from May 31st to June 1st.

Near the end of June the unit was ordered back towards Washington, D.C., to take part in General Philip Sheridan's Shenandoah Valley Campaign from August to October where it saw action in the Battle of Cedar Creek.

The Battle of Cedar Creek, Virginia on October 19, 1864 was one of the final, and most decisive, though expensive in casualties, battles in the Valley Campaigns of 1864. The Confederate invasion of the North, led by Lt. Gen. Jubal A. Early, was effectively ended. The Confederacy was never again able to threaten Washington, D.C. through the Shenandoah Valley. The South could also not protect its economic base. This victory aided the re-election of Abraham Lincoln as President and won lasting fame for Sheridan.

Incidentally, Pvt. Levi C. Clark, 10th Michigan Infantry noted in his diary on November 8, 1864:

*"Started at daylight. passed a little town called Cassville. Marched 15 miles. Camped on a piece of oakwood. Election, Michigan Soldiers permitted to vote. After noon showery."*

Unfortunately, Ephriam Roberts, after exemplary service with the 5th, was killed in action at the Battle of Cedar Creek, Virginia on October 19, 1864, one of 5,665 Union casualties.

Ami wrote a letter to his superiors requesting 20 days leave because his wife was very sick and

*"On the 19th of October last my only brother a member of the 5th Mich. Cav. was killed at the Battle of Cedar Creek, Va, whose business matters at home in which I am connected are in an unsettled condition and require my personal attention."*

The leave was granted.

**Bugler at lower right. (Brady photo, National Archives)**

Every army unit needs a bugler. The bugle was essential to all military communication during the Civil War. The primary bugler was assigned to the headquarters staff, and kept close to the commander at the front. Soldiers soon learned the meaning of each bugle call, and on an average day at least four, and sometimes as many as ten, were heard.

The Andrews Sisters made the bugler famous with their World War II song "Boogie Woogie Bugle Boy."

The 10th Michigan Infantry had its bugler in the person of Almonter Ami M. Roberts.

Roberts' enlistment paper listing "musician" as occupation (National Archives)

Ami was born in Erie County, New York on September 6, 1836, the eldest of four children born to John and Mariah Roberts. John moved the family to Almont in the 1844, when Ami was eight years old, and opened a general merchandise store. Ami hired on as clerk at the store at age fifteen while he was also learning the wagon-making trade. In addition, he played in a local band.

On Christmas Day, 1861 Ami enlisted in the Army in Almont as a sergeant. He stood 5' 11" tall (the average man stood 5' 7" in the 1860s). He had dark brown, almost black hair, dark brown eyes and a ruddy, dark complexion. Interestingly, he listed his profession as "musician" on his enlistment paper.

On October 6, 1861, shortly before his joining the Army and while assisting his uncle as postmaster in Goodland, Michigan, he married Harriet A. Clark. Ami had married Mary Phelps in April, 1858 but she died in Almont on August 22, 1860.

The 10th, with 27 Almonters, moved out on April 22, 1862 under the command of Colonel Charles M. Lum. (The community of Lum, Michigan in Arcadia Township, Lapeer County was named after Col. Lum in 1884.)

They joined the Army of the Cumberland in the Western Theater under Major General Henry W. Halleck in Pittsburg Landing, Tennessee. They saw Confederates immediately and participated in a number of skirmishes as well as built trenches and fortifications.

On September 10th, the unit marched to Nashville. They built more fortifications, guarded trains, etc., where the unit did suffer a few losses. Later the regiment was at Bridgeport, Alabama and crossed the Tennessee River near Chattanooga to Chickamauga Station. The men of the 10th always seemed to be in motion.

On February 6, 1864, 335 men mustered out and then re-enlisted in the regiment as veterans at Rossville, Georgia, including Sgt. Roberts.

Because of his organizational skills stemming from his days working in his father's store before the war, he was promoted from musician to full Quartermaster Sergeant in February 1864 and on December 31, 1864 Roberts was promoted to First Lieutenant and Full Quartermaster. That was a very big and important post for a man to hold.

In his report Quartermaster general, Brigadier General Montgomery C. Meigs wrote:

*"The quartermaster's department is charged with the duty of providing the means of transportation by land and water for all the troops and all the material of war. It furnishes the horses for artillery and cavalry, and for the trains; supplies tents, camp and garrison equipage, forage, lumber, and all materials for camps; builds barracks, hospitals, wagons, ambulances; provides harness, except for artillery horses; builds or charters ships and steamers, docks and wharves; constructs or repairs roads, bridges, and railroads; clothes the army; and is charged generally with the payment of all expenses attending military operations which are not expressly assigned by law or regulation to some other department."*

At Buzzards Roost, near Dalton, Georgia on February 25, 1864 the 10th found the Confederates and pushed toward their fortifications. They met a storm of cannon fire causing a loss of 13 killed, 35 wounded and 17 missing. Buzzards Roost was the most severe action the 10th encountered during the war.

After a 30 day furlough in Detroit, the regiment went back to Georgia and Tennessee and took part in the siege of Atlanta. The 10th was part of General Sherman's March to the Sea. They engaged the enemy at Savannah, Georgia and the North Carolina towns of Fayetteville, Averysboro, Bentonville, Raleigh, Goldsboro and on to the Southern Capital of Richmond, Virginia which had fallen into Union hands with the surrender of General Robert E. Lee at Appomattox Court House, Virginia on April 9, 1865.

The troops then went to Washington, D.C. and participated in the Grand Review in front of President Andrew Johnson, who had succeeded Lincoln after his assassination. Then it was on to Louisville, Kentucky where the regiment was mustered out of service on July 19th.

In all the 10th, of a total force of 1,514 men, lost 62 killed, 26 wounded, 9 died in Confederate prisons, 86 died of disease and

The Grand Review of troops VIP stand with Gen. U.S. Grant, Sec. of War Edwin Stanton, President Andrew Johnson, Gen. William T. Sherman, Gen. George Meade, cabinet members and other dignitaries. (Brady photo, National Archives)

178 were discharged because of severe wounds. This amounted to nearly 28% casualties.

Almonters William H. Watson, William R. Reed and Justice Hedges were among those who perished.

After the war, Ami came back to Almont and signed on as bookkeeper, foreman and collector for Currier, Moses and Company, which later became H. A. Currier & Bro. He and Harriet had three children, one boy and two girls. He was active in civic affairs in Almont, having been once elected a village trustee and served on many boards.

Lieutenant Roberts was present when the Liberty Pole was dedicated in downtown Almont in honor of the returning soldiers. I wonder if he played the bugle?

In 1877, Roberts moved to Detroit where he passed away on August 19, 1890. Mrs. Roberts survived until January 19, 1911. He rests in Woodmere Cemetery, Detroit.

The Roberts boys were two Almonters who had answered the call to duty.

# Lt. William B. Hamilton, Teacher, 22nd Michigan Infantry

Prisoner of war. Three words dreaded by every soldier who ever served. Almont's William B. Hamilton dreaded it, too, but unfortunately, he was held captive for 17 months as a POW in Rebel prisons.

Hamilton was born in Paisley, Scotland on September 23, 1831, son of William B. Sr. and Jean Downie. The Hamiltons moved from Scotland to a farm in Section 31, Berlin Township, just east of Almont, the area known as the Scotch Settlement. Young William went to school in a one room schoolhouse and was an excellent student. When he was twenty-one he began to teach others. He continued his education at the Dickinson Institute in Romeo and the Union School in Ann Arbor in preparation for attending the University of Michigan.

William B. Hamilton (Michigan State Archives)

However, with the onset of Civil War, Hamilton interrupted his studies and enlisted in Company B, 22nd Michigan Infantry on August 8, 1862 as a sergeant. His education was quickly recognized by the army and he was promoted to Second Lieutenant on June 5, 1863 and First Lieutenant on November 17, 1863 after being transferred to Company F.

Before he left for war, however, he married his sweetheart, Sara R. Stone in Rochester on August 29th.

The 997 men of the 22nd left for Kentucky on September 4, 1862 under the command of former Michigan Governor Moses Wisner. He contracted typhoid fever on the way to Kentucky and died in January 1863 and was succeeded by Col. Heber LeFavour.

The 22nd was in the Western Theater of the war operating mostly in Kentucky, Tennessee, Alabama and Georgia.

The Battle of Chickamauga, fought September 19–20, 1863, marked the end of a Union offensive in southeastern Tennessee and northwestern Georgia called the Chickamauga Campaign. The battle was the most significant Union defeat in the Western Theater of the American Civil War and the battle with one of the highest number of casualties in the war.

In her *History of the 22nd Michigan,* editor Susan Sridharan wrote:

*"The two armies finally clashed on September 19 in a wooded, hilly, middle-of-nowhere spot near Chickamauga Creek. The 22nd Michigan, being reinforcements, tensely listened to the sounds of battle from behind the lines near Rossville and wondered when their turn would come."*

Part of the Chickamauga Battlefield (Brady photo, National Archives)

When September 20th dawned, the fight resumed. Union General Gordon Granger became alarmed when sounds from the battle indicated a failing Union line. As the men were lining up for breakfast, he ordered "Double quick to the relief of General Thomas!" and they were off to battle with empty stomachs.

At 1:00 pm, after hurrying several miles over rough ground, they reported to Gen. Thomas just as Confederate forces were about to overrun part of Snodgrass Hill and break through the Union line. On the command of "Fix Bayonet! Charge Bayonet!" the 22nd, as part of Whitaker's Brigade, charged the hill and with heavy losses took possession. For over four hours the Confederates vainly tried to re-take the hill, but the 22nd Michigan, with the 89th Ohio and 21st Ohio, fought them off. By early evening the 22nd was out of ammunition and had to scavenge what they could from the bodies of the dead and wounded.

At a reunion of the 22$^{nd}$ ten years later, according to an article in the Detroit Post on September 2, 1875, Hamilton addressed his comrades. He described the death of his friend:

*"Nor must I forget my friend Joel H. Canfield* [23 year-old from Mt. Clemens, MI] *whose death affected me more than all the rest. One of the best boys, he was from my own Co. F universally loved and respected for his integrity and intelligence, a model soldier, a true Christian patriot. He was pierced by a ball in his left breast while kneeling in the act of firing, and rolled back almost at my feet, the life blood gushing from the wound and from his nose and mouth also. His last words to me were: 'Lieutenant, have I done my duty?' On being assured that he had, he said: 'Well I trust in Jesus; I'm going to a better home.' It was with utmost difficulty he could say even that; he was then carried off and I saw him no more."*

To most of the soldiers war was no longer an adventure. Hamilton said in his address:

*"This being under fire is a curious thing; it causes a feeling that is neither easily imagined nor described. To hear the balls go 'zip, zip' all around you, not knowing but the next one may make a different sound by coming in contact with your corporosity, is anything but soothing to the nerves. For myself, I have been in several places both before and since, where I would rather be than under fire. I have heard a good deal about soldiers spoiling for a fight, but my candid opinion is that a great many more fine fellows have been spoiled by fighting than for want of it."*

As it got dark, the 22$^{nd}$ made an unnerving discovery. While they had been holding the Confederates back, the rest of the Union army had taken the opportunity to retreat towards Chattanooga. By the time the 22$^{nd}$ Michigan realized they had been abandoned, it was too late to withdraw and they were surrounded. In the confused darkness, some of the men managed to play dead or roll into the bushes and hide, but almost everyone else was captured. Libby and Andersonville Prisons awaited them. Hamilton, Col. LeFavour and many others were among them.

*April 8th Friday*

No prisoners going today;— don't understand it. Rumors are rather adverse to exchange; but I see nothing very discouraging. Surg Doctor of the 73th Illinois came in today. He reports terrible suffering among our men at Andersonville Ga. Among the 7300 there are only about 200 shirts & 300 blankets the men being robbed or obliged to sell them for food. They have no shelter whatever, & are dying at the rate of 150 per week. He saw 21 corpses laid in a row—all had died in one day.

**Page from Hamilton's diary (courtesy Hamilton family)**

For the next seventeen months, Hamilton kept a diary while in Confederate prisons, a copy of which the author was given by Almonter Norm Hamilton, William's great grandson. A copy of the entire diary can be seen at the Almont District Library. In his entry for Sept.20th, Sunday, he writes:

> *"At 9 am ordered to reinforce Gen. Thomas. At 1 ½ pm came under fire. Opposed to Gen. Preston. Lost hearty & was taken prisoner."*

William B. Hamilton was an optimist. Throughout the diary, he talks about and is hopeful for an exchange of prisoners that might include him. A number of entries are similar to this one of December 20, 1863:

> *"Rumors of exchange seem to increase. Very cold."* But he also paints a picture of hell. Dec. 31: *"Am suffering for want of blankets – cold is quite severe…What a place to celebrate New Years!"*

March 14, 1864:

> *"Exchange all right. [Sic] 40 officers and 500 men were sent north today. Gen. Dow, Capts Sawyer & Flynn of retaliation notoriety are amongst them. When will my turn come?"*

Meanwhile, the war went on. The North was on the offensive but couldn't finish the job. Hamilton, while still hoping for an exchange, read books and taught himself German.

Lt. Hamilton spent most of his POW time in Libby Prison in Richmond. While it was anything but comfortable, it was nowhere near as bad as Andersonville Prison. On April 8 Hamilton wrote:

> *"…Doctor from the 73rd Illinois came in today. He reports terrible suffering among our men at Andersonville, Ga. Among the 7300, there are only 200 shirts & 300 blankets, the men being robbed or obliged to sell them for food. They*

*have no shelter whatever & are dying at a rate of 150 per week. He saw 21 corpses laid in a row – all had died in one day."*

**Libby Prison, Richmond, Virginia (Brady photo, National Archives)**

Later, as the Union forces came closer and closer to Richmond, he was moved several times to prisons in Danville and Macon, Georgia, Greensboro, North Carolina and Charlottesville, Virginia.

News of the war, however, did catch up to the prisoners from papers and various other sources. But mail from home was harder to come by. On September 18, 1864 he wrote:

*"Mead & Andrews got letters from home – also Spaulding. Surely it will be my turn next. My last news from home was dated the 17th of March I believe! God knows how I long to hear from my poor, dear Sara."*

Also on September 18th, he received news that he had been promoted to 1st Lieutenant. On the 20th Hamilton wrote:

*"This is the anniversary of the unlucky battle of Chickamauga in consequence of whose disastrous result I am here today. No one that has not experienced it can realize the amount of suffering crowded into one year's captivity."*

His hopes for exchange or release ebbed and flowed almost daily. Christmas came and went. New Years Day came and went. January and February 1865 came and went.

But, finally, on March 1, 1865, after 17 months of captivity, William became a free man again. His diary reads:

*"March the 1st is marked as an era in my life. On that glorious day I passed through the lines & stood once more under the Star Spangled Banner."*

The diary ends shortly after that entry. He had survived. Lee surrendered to Grant at Appomattox Court House, Virginia on April 9. The war was over.

In June, Lt. Hamilton was honorably mustered out and came home to Michigan and Sara. He enrolled in the medical school at the University of Michigan in Ann Arbor and became Doctor William B. Hamilton. He set up his practice in Burnside but returned to Almont in 1877. He and Sara had five children. He was elected to the post of Lapeer County Treasurer.

Dr. Hamilton continued to be active in civic affairs and was admired by the people who knew him and he attended many Veterans reunions. He died on November 1, 1918. His beloved Sara never remarried and died in Almont on November 27, 1927.

In the 1904 book *Michigan Poets and Poetry,* in which a dozen of his poems are printed, it states about Hamilton:

Gen. George H. Thomas "The Rock of Chickamauga" (Brady photo, National Archives)

*"Ever since childhood he has had a penchant for rhyming, a good deal of his work appearing in various local newspapers. Occasionally a piece would stray as far as New York or Philadelphia. He is best known as the author of poem 'The Rock of Chickamauga' which was first printed in the Detroit Post in 1875..."*

In the Post article Hamilton said:

*"In Schumaker's History of the War, Gen. Thomas is called the 'Rock of Chickamauga.' We old soldiers knew how well he merited the title. It struck me as having poetry in it and so I have made it the basis of my poem."*

### The Rock of Chickamauga

Let rebels boast their Stonewall brave
Who fell to fill a traitor's grave,
We have a hero grander far,
The Union was his guiding star,
The "Rock of Chickamauga."

When foot by foot, stern Rosecrans
Round grim Lookout, with bold advance,
Pressed back the rebels from their lair,
Our Thomas was the foremost there,
The "Rock of Chickamauga."

And when, in mightier force, they came
With serried ranks and sheets of flame,
Sweeping apart our shattered bands,
Who snatched the palm from rebel hands?
The "Rock of Chickamauga."

All day they surged and stormed in vain,
Lost Chattanooga to regain,

# Answering the Call to Duty

In vain each furious battle shock;
They were but waves, and he the rock,
The "Rock of Chickamauga."

His clarion voice with cheering word,
Above the din of battle heard,
His bearing firm, his kindling eye
Fired every breast with ardor high,
The "Rock of Chickamauga."

A new Thermopylae we found
On Chickamauga's bloody ground;
And in that rugged mountain pass
He stood our true Leonidas,
The "Rock of Chickamauga."

Sons of Macomb and broad St. Clair,
And Oakland's rolling fields were there.
And now they tell, with patriot pride,
How that great day they fought beside,
The "Rock of Chickamauga."

Gone is our hero, strong, and brave,
Columbia weeps above his grave,
While high upon the roll of fame,
She writes that loved and honored name,
The "Rock of Chickamauga."

—William B. Hamilton

(Lieut., 22nd Michigan Infantry, Co. F)

He also wrote this about his beautiful bride, Sara.

### After Eighteen Years

'Tis eighteen years to-day, dear wife,
Since first you owned that name,
Yet now, in the decline of life,
Our love remains the same.

Your face, though marked with lines of care
Your tresses — silvered o'er —
The same old charm still lingers there,
As in the days of yore.

Grim war stood by when we were wed.
And tore me from your side;
Three years in doubt and danger sped
Ere I reclaimed my bride.

Since then full many a heavy cross
Our weary limbs have borne,
And twice life's saddest, sorest loss,
Our hearts were called to mourn.

And still stern labor rules our lot,
And wealth disdains our call,
Yet surely, we are not forgot
By Him who cares for all.

For happy love — for sweet babes three —
For troops of faithful friends,
For wants supplied — oh God, to Thee
Our gratitude ascends!

Deemed by the world of low degree,

## Answering the Call to Duty

Sweetheart, we still can say,
I'm proud of you, and you of me,
As on our wedding day!
So, arm in arm, aglow with hope,
Our hearts as brave, as fond,
We'll wander down life's gentle slope
Nor fear what lies beyond.

Lt. William B. Hamilton, an Almonter who answered the call to duty.

# Birdseye McCullough, Farmer, 30th Michigan Infantry

Birdseye McCullough. I included him because I liked the name. I wonder if, when their precious baby boy came into the world, his parents, Thomas and Ann McCullough, looked

---

**STATE OF MICHIGAN,**

Town of _Ray_ _____ County of _Macomb_ _____

I, _Birdseye McCullough_ _____ born in _Oakland County,_

in the State of _Michigan_ _____ aged _17_ _____ years,

and by occupation a _Farmer_ _____, Do HEREBY ACKNOWLEDGE to have

volunteered this _Tenth_ _____ day of _December_ _____ 186 _4_,

to serve as a **SOLDIER IN THE ARMY OF THE UNITED STATES OF AMERICA**

for the period of _one year_ _____ unless sooner discharged by proper authority. Do also agree to accept such bounty, pay, rations and clothing, as are, or may be, established by law for volunteers. And I, _Birdseye McCullough_ do solemnly swear, that I will bear true faith and allegiance to the **UNITED STATES OF AMERICA**, and that I will serve them honestly and faithfully against all their enemies or opposers whomsoever; and that I will observe and obey the orders of the President of the United States, and the orders of the officers appointed over me, according to the Rules and Articles of War.

_Birdsey McCullough_

Sworn and subscribed to, at _Ray_

this _Tenth_ day of _December_ 186 _4_

BEFORE _Me Barlow Davis a_

_Notary Public in and for Macomb County_

**I CERTIFY ON HONOR,** That I have carefully examined the above named volunteer agreeably to the General Regulations of the Army, and that in my opinion he is free from all bodily defects and mental infirmity, which would, in any way, disqualify him from performing the duties of a soldier.

_Geo. Landon_

Examining Surgeon.

**I CERTIFY, ON HONOR,** That I have minutely inspected the volunteer _Birdsey McCullough_ previously to his enlistment, and that he was entirely sober when enlisted; that, to the best of my judgment and belief, he is of lawful age; and that, in accepting him as duly qualified to perform the duties of an able-bodied soldier, I have strictly observed the Regulations which govern the recruiting service. This soldier has _Blue_ eyes, _Brown_ hair, _Light_ complexion, is _five_ feet _6_ inches high.

_Mark Haughey_

_____ Regiment of Michigan Volunteers, (Infantry,)

_Capt._ RECRUITING OFFICER.

**Birdseye McCullough's Enlistment Form (National Archives)**

95

down at him and said, "He looks just like a Birdseye. That shall be his name."

Information about him is scarce but we do know that he grew up on his dad's farm near Ray, Michigan, just southeast of Almont and when he was seventeen, Birdseye, an only child, joined the Union army on December 10, 1864 for a one-year enlistment and was assigned to the 30th Michigan Infantry, Company B under thirty-one year old Captain William Bellis, from Chesterfield. (He's credited as an Almont enlistment).

His mother, for him to be accepted, had to sign a form that confirmed that he was seventeen and that *"I do hereby freely give my consent to his volunteering as a soldier in the army of the United States for the period of one year."*

The new soldier stood 5' 6" tall, had blue eyes and brown hair. He was paid $33.33 when he was mustered in on December 13th.

Because there was some uneasiness along the Canadian border, General Joseph "Fighting Joe" Hooker wrote to Secretary of War Edwin Stanton on November 3, 1864 that:

> *"Unless you can suggest some better mode of raising a regiment for service on the line from the foot of Lake Huron to Malden, I recommend that the authority be given to the Governor of Michigan to rise a volunteer Regiment for twelve months, unless sooner discharged. This additional force is necessary, and should be organized before the Detroit River is frozen over. No lesser force can render the frontier of Michigan secure from the incursion of the disaffected in Canada."*

Lame duck Michigan Governor Austin Blair, after Stanton's authorization, did just that. The 30th Michigan Infantry Regiment with 1,001 men was raised and made part of the U.S. Army on January 9, 1865.

The companies never left Michigan and were stationed at different points along the Detroit and St. Clair Rivers and in other parts of the State. Birdseye's Company B was stationed at Fort Gratiot which was an American stockade fort constructed in 1814 as an outpost to guard the juncture of the St. Clair River and Lake Huron, just north of Port Huron. Here they remained until they were mustered out in Detroit on June 30, 1865. None of the men in the regiment died in hostile action. Eighteen died of disease. There were no skirmishes against the Canadians.

Birdseye moved back to the farm and married his sweetheart, Angeline. When she died, he married the widow Rebeckah Corbin and adopted her two children. He lived out his life on a farm in Alaedion, Ingham County, Michigan.Birdseye, like so many other rural Michiganians, had answered the call to duty.

## Private Henry Dygert, Farmer, 16th Michigan Infantry

Twenty-seven year old Henry Dygert came to the United States from Ireland. He was a farmer. The 5' 8," blue eyed man joined the 16th Michigan Infantry Regiment, Company K (later transferred to Company B) at Almont on February 5, 1862.

The 16th, known as Stockton's Regiment for its commander, Col. Thomas B. Stockton, was one of the toughest and most controversial units in the war. It mustered in at Detroit on September 8, 1862 and mustered out in Jeffersonville, Indiana on July 8, 1865. It had a total of 2,318 officers and men with 10 officers and 155 men killed in action, 2 officers and 48 men died of wounds later and 128 men died of disease.

The 16th participated in 52 skirmishes and general engagements including 2nd Manassas, Antietam, Fredericksburg, Chancellorsville, Gettysburg, the Wilderness, Spotsylvania, Cold Harbor and Appomattox. The defeated Confederates surrendered some of their arms and battle flags to this regiment at Appomattox. Kim Crawford in his book *The 16th Michigan Infantry* says on page 533 that:

> *"While the surrender was solemn, Michigan soldiers who wanted souvenirs of the event made sure they got them. They later cut pieces out of the Rebel banners they received. 'Our regiment alone took thirteen flags,' Visscher wrote to his little sister. 'Lee's army gave their flags to our brigade. I send a small piece of two to you.'"*

Edward Hill of Company A, who would later be awarded the Medal of Honor at Cold Harbor, said

> *"...Where the black smoke of battle rolled heaviest, there could the 16th be found."*

98

On the second day of the battle of Gettysburg, July 2, 1863, the 16th was one of the key units in defending Little Round Top, high ground to the south of the battlefield. Sent to Little Round Top, Brig. Gen. Gouverneur K. Warren found only a small Signal Corps station on the hill. When he saw the glint of bayonets in the sun to the southwest he realized that a Confederate assault into the Union flank was imminent. He hurriedly sent staff officers to find help from any available units in the vicinity.

Col. Strong Vincent answered the call and upon arrival on Little Round Top, received fire from Confederate batteries almost

Little Round Top, Gettysburg in 1863 (Brady photo, National Archives)

immediately. On the western slope he placed the 16th Michigan, and then proceeding counterclockwise were the 44th New York, the 83rd Pennsylvania, and finally, at the end of the line on the southern slope, the 20th Maine.

The Confederates made several furious, sustained attacks up the hill in attempt to gain the high ground. Shortly the Union regiments on the hill were in dire straits. While the Alabamians had pressed their attacks on the Union left, the 4th and 5th Texas were attacking Vincent's 16th Michigan on the Union right. Rallying the crumbling regiment (the smallest in his brigade, with only 263 men) several times, Vincent was mortally wounded during one Texas charge.

In his book *The 16th Michigan Infantry*, Kim Crawford writes:

> *"Along the 16th Michigan's line, the combatants fired at each other from close range, and in some places were said to have fought with bayonets and clubbed muskets."*

The 16th took the brunt of the assaults and were much more exposed than other regiments as there were few boulders to offer cover near their position. Some of the men retreated toward the top of the hill. The controversy about why the men moved remains to this day. Did they retreat or run?

This author prefers to believe they wisely retreated to a better position to fight some more.

But in either case, Little Round Top remained in Union hands, one of the decisive actions in the Battle of Gettysburg.

At some time during this fierce fighting, Almont's Henry Dygert was killed in action, one of twenty-three officers and men from the 16th killed that day.

Henry Dygert's bravery and love for the Union can never be questioned. He answered the call to duty.

# Levi C. Clark,  Farmer,  10th Michigan Infantry

*February 28, 1864*

> *"Started from home. Stopped at Romeo and stayed all night."*

*February 29, 1864*

> *"Went to Pontiac. Was examined. Past [sic] muster. Stayed till March first."*

*March 2, 1864*

> *"Started at eleven and a half at night to go to Grand Rapids. Got there at 10 next morning and went into camp. Next day was detailed to draw water."*
>
> –Levi C. Clark

Sometimes it's difficult to write a profile of a Civil War soldier, at least the part about what he did continually during his service. His war record in the National Archives may only say "Nov-Dec, 1864 Present." There is not much detail but Almonter Levi C. Clark gives us a very detailed account of his service. He kept a daily diary beginning February 28, 1864 up to April 2, 1865. Above are the first three days of the diary. The re-written transcript of the entire diary can be seen at the Ruth Hughes Memorial District Library in Imlay City, Michigan.

Clark enlisted in Company F, 10th Michigan Infantry in Almont on February 29, 1864 (leap year). He was a 38 year-old farmer who stood 5' 8" tall, had blue eyes, dark hair and a light complexion according to his enlistment paper.

The 10th left Michigan on April 22nd and proceeded to the Western Theater of the war primarily in Tennessee. It saw some action against the Rebels with the loss of nearly 20 men killed.

Private Clark was in training camp in Grand Rapids throughout March. The following is from March 7th.

*"Pleasant morning. Called out in the fore noon and drilled again. After noon drilled again and marched out of the yard. Then had to sweep the yard."*

*March 27.*

*Foggy this morning but came off warm and pleasant. Went down to the creek and had a good wash."*

Company F stayed in training camp in Grand Rapids until April 1st, often enduring up to four inches of snow. On the 1st, Clark's diary entry reads:

*"Started from Grand Rapids. Went to Detroit. Got there at eight at night. Marched down though the city to the Rail way depot...but would not go..."*
*"Apri. 2 Reported to Col. Lum at nine o'clock in the morning. Went to the cars (railroad) and came to Fentonville. Took the stage from there to the Flint. Stayed that night. Reported at 9 o'clock to the Captain. Got furlough to come home. Started at 11 o'clock. Came to Barrieses Corner. Stayed all night and at 11 o'clock started from there for home where I arrived about 4 o'clock. Found all well and glad to see me."*

The entire 10th Regiment was given a furlough on March 1st, April 20th it was back to business. Clark and his unit traveled for three days on the train, passing though Fentonville, Pontiac, Detroit, Kalamazoo, Niles, Indianapolis and finally arrived at Nashville, Tennessee on April 23rd.

Starting April 27th, the regiment marched and marched some more. The entry for the 27th:

*"Started from Nashville. Marched about 9 miles. Camped on a high ridge. A most splendid country."*

They marched daily until they reached Georgia. According to the diary, they covered 209 miles until May 15th.

**Union enlisted men, like Clark, relax in camp before the next march. (Brady photo, National Archives)**

*"Marched 12 miles. Passed within about a mile where there was fighting. Camped in a piece of woods within hearing of the fighting. Was called up about 12 o'clock to prepare to march but did not go."*

This was Pvt. Clark's first sound of hostile fire but certainly not his last. On May 17th, there *"was a skirmishing."* On the 18th: *"Marched a mile and a half and drove the enemy across the river."* It was often a long time between baths for the men and washing their clothes. On May 21st, Clark first mentions washing his shirts and socks. Then it was more marching, scores of miles until May 29th:

*"Sunday. Lay in line of battle all day. Kept up the firing on the skirmish line all day. Had a fight. Killed, wounded and*

The 10th Infantry would like this in camp. (Brady photo, National Archives)

*taken prisoners, 1,500 men. Moved about 40 rods. (Author's note: a rod = 16.5 feet) Lay in line of battle - fighting through the night. Lay within 40 rods of the cannon. Rebel losses estimated at 2,000. Our killed 40, 100 wounded."*

This action was part of the Siege of Atlanta. On June 24th this very close call:

*"Day very warm. Lying behind breastwork. The balls keep whistling over head. A ball passed through the skirt of my blouse right by my hip when I was standing in front of tent. Went on picket at night."*

And on the 29th:

*"Lay behind breast work. Went in front and saw them bury their dead. A most melancholy sight. Our loss in killed and wounded estimated 790. Bradford, cook to Co. E, died from a wound coming in where we are now. Our Colonel is sick.*

*Sour kraut for dinner. A little extra! Rebels made a charge on us but without effect."*

So it went. Marching, camping, drilling, foraging, fighting. On July 7th he got a chance to wash his clothes as he did again on August 26th . On July 16th he describes his gear:

*"Had to be ready at 6 o'clock with accounterments [sic] and haver sack, napsack [sic], canteen for general inspection."*
*"July 20. Lay there all day in a hot sun. 4 of our company wounded and one killed. Falmon H. Owens was hit in left arm and W. Bradley in the hip. John Grinnel in both legs but John slightly. I lay between him and Falmon when they were hit."*
*"Aug. 13. Morning foggy. Cleared off. A drummer was killed today."*
*"Aug. 24. Very hot. Drew rations. Lay in camp. One of the Payton boys over."*

Brothers John and David Payton, 22nd Michigan Infantry, were friends from Almont.

Conditions for soldiers were often terrible. For example, he writes on October 5th:

*"Rainy morning. Marched in rain, mud and water ankle deep. Forded Elk River ov 80 rods across."*
*"Oct. 22. Foggy and cold. Started out at daylight. Made a halt and stacked arms. Marched 10 miles. Camped in an open field. Put up our tents in regular order. Went out foraging for potatoes. Did not get any. Blistered my feet marching."*

On November 8th he notes:

*"Election. Michigan soldiers permitted to vote."*

This was the re-election of President Lincoln.

The 10th Michigan Infantry was part of General William Tecumseh Sherman's famous March to the Sea that began on November 15th and ended in Savannah on December 21st. All along the way, Sherman's army lived off the land and destroyed everything in its path. On Nov. 16th Clark notes:

A Union soldier on lonely picket duty (Brady photo, National Archives)

*"Left Atlanta at 11 0'clock. Burnt the city before leaving..."*
Later (Feb 18, 1865) he writes:

*"The army burns houses, barns, fences and almost all they cannot carry away. Some women crying, others laughing. I felt sorry."*

The next entries describe the marching, the food (parched corn, beans, coffee, potatoes and some chicken) and more daily life along the March. On December 27th he says:

*"Clear and warm. Marched to Savannah. Reviewed by General Sherman...Savannah is a fine city. Streets well laid out and shaded."*

The unit then marched into South Carolina and North Carolina. On March 30th, Clark was detailed to General Henry Slocum's staff. The diary ends on April 2, 1865, a week before Lee surrendered to Grant on April 9th and 12 days before the President was assassinated. He wrote:

*"Sunday. Warm. Oh how glad I should feel to be at home and take a walk as we used to."*

Private Levi C. Clark was honorably discharged on December 19, 1865 and returned to Michigan. He lived on his farm in Almont until his death on April 29, 1902. He had answered the call to duty.

Levi C. Clark's final resting place, Webster Cemetery, Imlay City, Michigan (author photo)

## The Justin Brothers
### Capt. William, Corp. Isaac, Pvt. Alonzo, Pvt. Clark, Pvt. George

The Civil War is often referred to as the war that pitted brother against brother. That was true in many, many cases especially in border states where it was not uncommon for families to be split in their loyalties with some men wearing blue while a sibling wore grey. One well-known case, for example, was the Crittenden brothers of Kentucky. The father, John J. Crittenden, was a state legislator, Governor of Kentucky, Attorney General of the United States and a United States Senator. Although a slave owner, Sen. Crittenden believed in preserving the Union and remained loyal to the Northern cause. His sons, however, were split.

Thomas, a lawyer, supported the Union and joined the army in September, 1861. In July, 1862, he was promoted to Major General, leading his troops in battle at Shiloh, Perryville, Stone's River and Chickamauga.

Older brother George, on the other hand, also a lawyer and graduate of West Point, resigned his commission and joined the Confederate Army and by November, 1861 he also was a Major General assigned to liberate Kentucky.

Both brothers survived the war and later served in Kentucky government.

Far more common during the war was brother fighting with brother on the same side, often in the same unit. General George Armstrong Custer's brother, Thomas, served in the Union Army, the last year as his brother's aide-de-camp. Tom Custer was awarded two Medals of Honor for his gallantry. Unfortunately, Tom followed his brother later and died alongside him at the Battle of the Little Bighorn in 1876.

Colonel Joshua Lawrence Chamberlain, famous leader known for his daring downhill bayonet attack with the 20th Maine regiment on Little Round Top at Gettysburg stopping the Confederate attack of the 15th Alabama, served with his brother, Thomas, in the 20th throughout the war.

Earlier in this book we profiled the Roberts brothers, Ephriam and Ami from Almont.

The Justin brothers were brought to my attention by Almont High School student, Justin Demo. Justin's great-grandfather, Ralph Justin, was my neighbor as I grew up in Almont and Ralph's grandfather, Clark O. Justin, was one of the brothers, all residents of St. Clair County, in the Civil War.

According to family historian, Don Justin, there have been Justins in military service all the way back to 1675 when John Justin served in the Rhode Island Militia during King Philip's War, a bloody armed conflict between Native Americans and English settlers. Several Justins served in the French and Indian War.

Charles Justin of Canterbury, Connecticut served in the American Revolutionary War as a Minuteman in response to the alarm at Lexington and was in the 1st Connecticut Line at Valley Forge, Princeton and Yorktown. Gershum and Walcot Justin, both from Whiting Township, Vermont also served in the Revolutionary War. All three were wounded in action. Don also tells us that as many as seven Justins were in the War of 1812.

Justins also served with distinction in the Civil War, the Spanish American War, World Wars I and II, Korea, Vietnam and Iraq.

In addition there have been two navy ships named *USS Justin*. The first was a steamship, converted from a schooner, commissioned in 1898 and assigned to carry and deliver coal for other ships and stations. She was decommissioned in 1915 as most of the navy had switched to oil to power ships. The second was a former Liberty Ship renamed and commissioned in September, 1945, that served as a troop transport in the Pacific. She was decommissioned in 1946.

### Civil War

There were five Justin brothers who served in the Union Army during the American Civil War. All of them were the sons of Alonzo Lee Justin and his wife, Sarah Hollenbeck. Alonzo's mother,

Polly Chaffee Justin Bowman had moved with her second husband, William W. Bowman from New York to a farm in St. Clair Township, Michigan in 1834 bringing young Alonzo with her.

Polly, the family matriarch, had ten grandsons serve in the war. In addition to the five Justin men, there were four Chaffee men and one Bowman. George Bowman joined the 4th Michigan Infantry while Amasa Chaffee was in the 1st Michigan Light Artillery; Edward A. Chaffee joined the Michigan Engineers and Construction Corps. Phillip A. Chaffee and Theron Chaffee were both part of the 1st Michigan Light Artillery, Battery H. There were also twelve in-laws that served.

**Artillery battery at the ready (Brady photo, National Archives)**

## William H. Justin

After the start of the war and Governor Blair's call for troops, 23 year-old William Justin was the first of the brothers to sign up. William was very tall for the time, standing 6 feet 3½ inches tall with hazel eyes and light brown hair. He loved chopping wood and rafting and listed himself as a lumberman on his enlistment form. In his youth he is said to have cleared the timber from 100 acres of land.

William joined the 1st Michigan Light Artillery on November 15, 1861.

*"The Regiment of the Michigan Light Artillery was composed of twelve six gun batteries. They were commanded by Colonel C.O. Loomis, but from the character of that arm of the service, the batteries were never brought together as a unified Regiment,"* www.michiganinthewar.org, Don Harvey.

Units tried to ensure that all six guns in a battery were of the same caliber, simplifying training and logistics. Each piece, as the guns were referred to, was operated by a gun crew of eight men, plus four additional men to handle the horses and equipment.

Six horses were required to move a piece from one place to the other. The team of horses was hitched to a limber, a two wheeled carriage that carried an ammunition chest with the cannon or caisson, another two wheeled cart attached behind it. Sometimes a second team carried the caisson which was loaded with more ammunition, ramrods, fuses, extra horseshoes, a portable forge and

**Artillery on the move (Brady photo, National Archives)**

other equipment needed for the mission. The combination of gun and carriage weighed thousands of pounds so horses usually served for only a few months.

Each two-piece section of the battery was commanded by a lieutenant while the six-gun battery was led by a captain.

Battery H, with Private Justin along, was mustered into federal service in Monroe, Michigan on March 6, 1862 and left the

**Eight man gun crew (Brady photo, National Archives)**

state under the command of Captain Samuel DeGolyer of Hudson, Michigan on March 13th. The unit was attached to the Artillery Division of the Army of the Mississippi in July 1862. In September, William was wounded in the left hip by friendly fire when a pistol held by 2nd Lieut. Edmund M. Luce of the same unit accidentally discharged with the bullet being lodged in his hip for the rest of his life.

Battery H was engaged in battle at Thompson Hills, Vicksburg, Raymond, Jackson, Champion Hill, Brownsville and Clinton, Mississippi as well as Big Shanty, Kennesaw, Nickajack Creek, Peach Tree, Atlanta, Jonesboro and Lovejoy's Station in Georgia.

Captain William H. Justin (courtesy Justin family)

DeGolyer's Battery drew praise for its action at the battle of Raymond by newspaperman and author Horace Greeley.

*"The rebels opened... attempting to charge and capture DeGolyer's battery but being repulsed by a terrific fire of grape and canister, they broke and fled precipitately."*

(Grape and canister rounds from a cannon act like giant shotgun shells scattering deadly metal shards from the canister and iron or steel balls in a wide swath taking out many advancing infantry troops.)

Private Justin's leadership qualities were recognized early in his enlistment and he was promoted to Corporal, First Sergeant, 2nd Lieutenant, 1st Lieutenant and finally Brevet Captain.

On September 15, 1863 from Vicksburg, Brig. Gen. M. D. Leggett wrote the following letter to Michigan Governor Austin Blair:

*"The captaincy in DeGolyer's Battery (8ᵗʰ Mich) having become vacant by the death of the gallant and patriotic DeGolyer, please permit me to recommend that 1ˢᵗ Lieut. Jacob L. Richmond of said battery be promoted to the Captaincy. Also 2ⁿᵈ Lieut. Marcus D. Elliott to 1ˢᵗ Lieut. And First Sergeant Wm. Justin to 2ⁿᵈ Lieutenant. These officers are all excellent men and in camp, on the march and on many bloody battlefields have shown themselves capable and highly worthy of the promotions asked. The standing & reputation of DeGolyer's Battery is second to none in Grant's Army."*

After being promoted again to 1ˢᵗ Lieutenant, Justin and the battery also fought at the Battle of Lovejoy's Station, Georgia during the Atlanta campaign. Below is Lieut. Justin's report:

IN THE FIELD, near Lovejoy's Station, September 4, 1864.

*In accordance with instructions from superior headquarters, I have the honor to report the following rebel casualties (as far as it was possible to ascertain them) in our front on the 31st ultimo and 1st instant:*

*During the charge made upon the Fifteenth Corps on the 31st I kept up a steady fire, concentrating upon a rebel battery, which was covering the advance of their lines. This firing is represented by officers in the Fifteenth Corps to have been of great service in breaking the ranks of the enemy and destroying the vehemence of his attack.*

*September 1, the battery held a commanding position, from which a rapid and well-directed fire of short-time fuse-shell was poured upon bodies of rebel troops distinctly seen retreating before the advance of the Fourteenth Corps, causing great confusion and demoralization among them. Upon the enemy's endeavoring to construct rail works to impede the advance of our forces I opened upon them with all six guns, rendering the work too hazardous to be continued. This done I concentrated their fire upon a battery close at hand. This I was unable to silence utterly by reason of its being in works. Its retreat, however, was made impossible, many of their horses having been killed and disabled by our shell. The battery was captured by our forces in the spot it had been firing from.*

*I take this opportunity to state that too great praise cannot be given the officers and men under me for the able manner in which they have invariably executed all commands given them, not only during these engagements but throughout the campaign. They have in many cases fought with no protection whatever, exposed to fire from the enemy's artillery and sharpshooters, never faltering not hesitating in the discharge of their duty.*

*I have no casualties to report in my command during the 31st of August and 1st of September.*

*All of which is respectfully submitted.*

*WILLIAM JUSTIN, First Lieutenant, Commanding Battery H, First Michigan Light Arty.*

Brevet Captain Justin was honorably discharged from his unit on December 31, 1864 at the end of his service agreement.

After the war William moved back to Michigan and resumed farming. He married Annie Haskell in 1864 and had two children with her, Sarah Ann and Estella. Annie died in 1872 and in 1873 he married Ellen Ervin in Sanilac County on September 27, 1873. Together they had nine more children, William, Bertha, Dorah, Margaret, Esther, John, Cora, Jimmie and Ella.

Captain Justin died on December 18, 1922. Ellen died on May 31, 1929. They rest together in Lakeside Cemetery, Port Huron, Michigan.

## Isaac Justin

William's 21 year-old brother Isaac joined the army as a private on August 5, 1862 and was mustered in to his brother's

Corporal Isaac JUSTIN and Private Henry COX of St. Clair twonship, taken circa 1862. Both were in Battery "H", 1st. Michigan Light Artillery also called the 8th Michigan Battery.

Corporal Isaac Justin (left) and Private Henry Cox (courtesy Justin family)

authors note: original spelling on photo

unit, Battery H, 1st Michigan Light Artillery (DeGolyer's Battery) in Detroit on August 10th for three years. Isaac, born December 31, 1840, stood six feet tall, had gray eyes, brown hair with a fair complexion and was a farmer.

Isaac suffered from measles and rheumatism and was confined to a hospital in Memphis, Tennessee and Milliken's Bend, Louisiana a good deal of time. Isaac, however, was by all accounts, a good soldier. He was promoted to Corporal on April 1, 1864. After the war in 1895, Marcus D. Elliott, former Captain of Battery H wrote to the Commissioner of Pensions in Washington, D.C. (letter on left). Corporal Justin was granted a disability pension after the war based upon this injury.

Isaac was discharged in July 1865 and moved back to St. Clair County where he married Mary V. Redfield on Dec. 30, 1866. She passed away on January 28, 1885. He married the widow Maria Louisa Hills (nee Moak) on April 24, 1887 in Port Huron. He died on October 14, 1917 and was joined in death by Maria on February 19, 1929. They are interred in St. Clair.

## Alonzo Lee Justin, Jr.

Alonzo Justin, Jr. was born on the family farm in St. Clair County on October 20, 1846. When the Civil War began and his

older brother, William, joined the army, 15 year-old Alonzo decided to do the same and lied about his age. Since he was almost six feet tall no one questioned him about it so he went with William to Battery H as a private in November 1861. Alonzo was a good soldier and in June or July 1862 he was granted leave. He never came back. The official Battery Muster Roll of September-October 1862 lists him as "Absent without leave." The November-December Muster Roll reads "Dropped from the

**Private Alonzo Justin, Jr.**
**(courtesy Justin family)**

**Alonzo Justin file, (National Archives)**

119

Marlette, Sanilac Co Mich
Nov 6, 1883
middle div
How John C Black
Regimal No 114075
Commr of Pensions
Sir
In regard to the Case of
Alonzo Justin whos Claim has been
rejected on the Ground of Desertion
that he was a deserter from Co H, 1st Mich
Light-Artilly—at the time he enlisted in Co H
8th Mich Cavalry—According to his statement
which is Corroborated by a number of persons
and soldiers of Co H 1st Mich Lgt Artilly — the facts
Are as follows Alonzo Justin Enlisted between the
age of 16 & 17 years and was taken out when
on furlough from New Madrid Mo—by his
Father—when past 18 years of age he enlisted
in Co H 8 Mich Cavalry and served until the
Close of the War and received an honorable
discharge which is on file in Your office
Alonzo Justin and his three Brothers who
served throughout the War think You have
done him an injustice in branding
One of them a deserter —Wm Justin
enlisted as private and Came out Capt
of Co H 8th Mich Battery — his soldier
friends whom I have heard speak

of the Matter all say a wrong has
been done Alonzo Justin in throwing
out his Claim on the point stated
in Your letter — I trust You will
reconsider this Case and do
justice to the party interested, he
and his soldier friends have confidence
in Your honesty and fairness I
hope they will have no reason for
changing this kindly feeling
hopeing to receive a reply I am
Very Respt Yours
P S
Robt Willis
The Hon E C Carleton of Port
Huron is acquainted with the
parties in this Case

**Alonzo Justin file, National Archives)**

Rolls for being absent without leave." And later a Muster Roll reads "Deserted."

Being a deserter is a very serious offense and can result in execution. There was nothing in Alonzo's background or his service as a soldier that would lead one to believe he would shirk his duty. It was a mystery.

After the war Alonzo had applied for a pension and was rejected for being a deserter but on further investigation an 1886 notation from the Adjutant General's Office reads, "The notations of May of 1884 are cancelled. He was discharged at Detroit, Mich July 13, 1863 on a writ of Habeas Corpus by reason of minority."

A letter to the Commissioner of Pensions by Robert Willis of Marlette dated November 6, 1885 clears up the mystery.

Alonzo's dad took him home to the farm but he didn't stay there. He knew his place was in the army so he reenlisted on February 3, 1864 in Co. H, 8th Michigan Cavalry. Army paperwork sometimes didn't catch up.

Clark O. Justin Enlistment form, (National Archives)

The 8th Michigan Cavalry was mustered into service on May 2, 1863 and was assigned to the Western Front seeing action in nearly 40 battles mostly in Kentucky, Tennessee and Georgia. Unfortunately, Private Justin was sick much of his time with the 8th Cavalry with diarrhea. Diarrhea afflicted many soldiers during the war due to the lack of clean drinking water and was especially hard on cavalry troops who spent much of their time in the saddle.

Justin was discharged on May 17, 1865 and eventually did receive his pension. Back in Michigan as a farmer and lumberjack he married his sweetheart, Fannie Gardner on March 13, 1870. They had six children together. Alonzo passed away on February 23, 1923 in Gladwin. Fannie followed him in death on February 17, 1929. They are buried in Highland Cemetery, Gladwin.

### Clark O. Justin

Clark's turn came on September 24, 1864. He was 18 years old, 5 feet 7 inches tall, had dark eyes, brown hair, a dark complexion and sported a long but trimmed beard. On his enlistment for his occupation he wrote "farmer."

He was assigned to Company I of the reorganized 4th Michigan Infantry and sent to the Western Front. The original 4th fought in the east at Fredericksburg, Antietam, Gettysburg, Chancellorsville, the Wilderness and the siege of Petersburg. After its term of enlistment expired it was mustered out of service on June 30, 1864. The following is taken from Don Harvey's website:

*"As soon as the original 4th was mustered out on June 30, 1864 one hundred and twenty-nine men re-enlisted as veteran volunteers and the Regiment was at once reorganized with eight new companies under Colonel Jairus W. Hall at Adrian.*

*The reorganized Fourth was mustered into United States service October 14, 1864, then on the 22nd left Adrian for Nashville, Tn. It was engaged with the Confederates at Decatur, Ala., and New Market, soon after being sent to*

Pvt. Clark O. Justin (courtesy Justin family)

*Huntsville, Al. where it was assigned to the Third Brigade, Third Division, Fourth Army Corp. In March the Regiment went by rail to Knoxville, Tn., then marched throughout East Tennessee, returning to Knoxville on April 27th. In June the Fourth was embarked upon transports and sent to New Orleans, La., where a detachment of re-enlisted veterans joined the Regiment. In July the Regiment was sent by transports to Indianola, Texas then marched to San Antonio. The Regiment remained in Texas until May 26, 1866, where it mustered out of service at Houston, returning to Detroit June 10, where it was paid off and disbanded."*

Private Justin mustered out with the rest of the 4th at Houston and his Muster Out Roll says *"retained one Springfield Rifle... $6.00"*.

Clark moved to a farm in St. Clair Township, Michigan and there married 18 year-old Emily Dunton on September 4, 1867. They had eight children. He died on November 7, 1910 in Burnside Township. Emily died on April 18, 1928. They were the grandparents of the author's neighbor, Ralph Justin, of Almont.

### George Justin

Nearly everyone who has ever read a history book in school is familiar with the image of the Civil War drummer boy. The drummer boy, usually aged between 10 and 14, was not just a mascot but was a very important part of a unit. He had to be able to tap out many

**Union drummer boys in camp (Brady photo, National Archives)**

different drum rolls as communication signals to the troops during a march, in camp and even in battle. In addition, when not drumming, the boys performed myriad other duties such as cooking, helping feed and water the horses, clean the tents and camp, run errands, clean weapons and do just about anything else they were told to do.

According to the family, George Justin, age 10, was a drummer boy for his brothers' unit, Battery H, 1$^{st}$ Michigan Light Artillery in 1864 and 1865. How he was able to leave the farm and join his brothers in war at such a young age with his father's knowledge is a mystery. He lies with other family members in Bowman Cemetery in St. Clair.

The Justins are a proud American family always ready to answer the call to duty.

# CHAPTER SEVEN

# THE LIBERTY POLE

**Almont's Liberty Pole, Dedicated July 4, 1865 (Almont District Library)**

A fter the war nearly every town in America erected some sort of a monument to its sons who served. There are countless statues, monuments, parks and other tributes in towns and villages all over Michigan.

Almont was no exception. But rather than a stone monument or bronze statue, Almont raised a Liberty Pole to honor the returning troops and as a memorial to those who couldn't return.

The pole was made from two white pine trees felled nearby. After the pine's arrival in Almont, craftsmen sawed and hand hewn

125

the logs into a magnificent flagpole. One section, made two feet wide at the base, was 80 feet long. The other was a foot wide at the base and tapered to about six inches. The two logs, with a ten foot splice to make the pole very sturdy, were bolted together, finished and painted.

A hole eight feet deep and three feet wide was dug in front of the bank at the corner of North Main and East St. Clair, the northeast corner of the four corners in the center of town. With good engineering, the pole was raised and rose 112 feet above Almont.

On the nation's 89th birthday, July 4, 1865, the pole was dedicated. Veterans such as Captain William Colerick, 1st Lt. Cornelius Croley, Lt. Melvin J. Fitch, Captain Charles E. Greble, 2nd Lt. Calvin M. Hall and Lieutenant Ami M. Roberts, all in full dress uniform, attended the event. Many of the enlisted men who had served were also present as well as civilian men in their Sunday best and ladies in their finery, on hand to mark the occasion. The band played, speeches were given and then Old Glory was raised to the top of the pole as the Almont Band played The Star Spangled Banner (not yet the official national anthem).

Later a 16 foot-in-diameter bandstand was built nearly 20 feet above the street from which the band played many concerts over the years.

The Liberty Pole watched over Almont until 1919 when it had deteriorated beyond repair and was taken down. It had served long and well as a salute to Almont's veterans of the Civil War and the civilians of the village who supported them in the war effort.

The same view in 2010. The Liberty Pole was just off the curb on the other side of street. (author photo)

# CHAPTER EIGHT

# THE TOWN AFTER THE WAR

After the guns fell silent, all of the parades were finished, the speeches made and the Liberty Pole was dedicated, Almont, like all small towns across Michigan and the country, tried to get back to "normal."

Some of the men had serious disabilities from wounds or disease suffered during the war and a lot of those, or their widows, were paid a pension by the federal government.

Most of the soldiers, however, returned to their homes, farms or businesses to pick up where they had left off, albeit in a much-changed nation. Ben Johnston returned and opened a furniture store. Ami Roberts served as bookkeeper for Currier, Moses and Company. William B. Hamilton went to medical school and became Dr. Hamilton. War Commissioner John B. Hough became Probate Judge. A chapter of the Grand Army of the Republic (GAR) was established in memory of Lt. Col. Melvin Brewer.

The South lay in ruins and its citizens faced Reconstruction which, after the assassination of President Lincoln, was harder and harsher. Most of the structures as well as the economy of the entire region had to be rebuilt. Some would argue that the former Confederate States have not recovered yet.

Though slavery was officially banned by the Thirteenth Amendment to the Constitution, the "Jim Crow" laws survived and the former slaves held second-class citizenship...or worse...until the 1960s in both the North and the South.

Almonters, of course, were active during the Spanish American War, World War I, World War II, Korea, Vietnam, Iraq and anywhere else the country needed them. Whenever the nation called, Almonters answered the call to duty and we all remain grateful for their service and sacrifice.

Progress back in Almont was slow but steady. The plank road was removed in 1869, replaced by a dirt road reinforced with gravel which didn't get as muddy. Roads paved with cement didn't appear until the 1920'.

The telegraph, used so effectively during the war, finally arrived in Almont in 1875. It made life easier for A.H. Patterson publisher of *The Almont Herald*. He could now report "up to the minute" news.

The Townsend and Currier Bank opened in 1870, the first of several "modern" banks.

But it wasn't until 1882 that Almont really began to grow and prosper. A branch of the Port Huron and Northwest Railroad was built connecting Almont with Port Huron.

**Almont west side Main Street looking southwest after the war (Almont District Library)**

Now the farmers and merchants could move their goods faster to Port Huron where they could be loaded onto ships and sent around the Great Lakes. The railroad ran until 1942.

**The railroad came to Almont in 1882 (Almont District Library)**

The first electric rail car (trolley car) rolled into Almont from Romeo and points south in July 1914. Now the farmers had a direct line to Detroit. The electric car ran until 1925. It was replaced by a daily Greyhound bus. The tracks were removed on 1929.

**Arrival of the first "Trolley Car" (Almont District Library)**

**The Almont – Romeo Bus (Almont District Library)**

As electricity came to Almont, the town and township grew even more. With the influx of trucks and automobiles, roads were paved and the people of the little town could now reach anywhere. In his 1930 letter to *The Almont Herald*, Ripley Shaw wrote:

*"As I look back over the intervening years and see the wonderful strides that have been made, I am amazed. Now the farmers nearly all have telephones, rural delivery, daily papers, trolley cars and flying through the air seems to be an accomplished fact. What will the next fifty years see?"*

As technology advanced everywhere, it advanced in Almont, too. The Victrola and then television and radio appeared and Detroit became a major broadcasting center. Automobile factories opened employing some Almonters. Automobile dealers opened and provided Almonters with the latest models. The Hurd Lock Company came to town, employing many more citizens. An airport opened. The volunteer fire department became one of the best in the state. Restaurants opened, churches grew, dances were enjoyed, music from local bands entertained, a movie theater opened, a "Homecoming" was established for every five years inviting all Almonters home.

The school was modernized and, after a fire, a new one was opened in 1928. Even more modern school buildings were added in the 1980s as the township grew and more children needed educating.

So Almont, our little hidden gem in the Thumb, continues to this day to grow "in the right direction" as the welcoming signs at the edge of town proclaim.

As Mr. Shaw asked, *"What will the next fifty years see?"* I'm sure Almont will still be here prospering ready to answer the call to duty.

**Almont Main Street looking southwest after the war (Almont District library)**

**Downtown Almont looking southwest, 2010 (author photo)**

# APPENDIX ONE

**These Sons of Almont gave what Abraham Lincoln called in the Gettysburg Address "the last full measure of devotion."**

**Pvt. Amos Beach**  Died of disease at Columbia, Tennessee, May 26, 1864

**Pvt. Eady F. Beach**  Died of disease at Bridgeport, Alabama, December 12, 1863

**Pvt. George Beach**  Died of disease at Nashville, Tennessee, January 15, 1865

**Lt. Col. Melvin Brewer**  Killed in action at Winchester, Virginia, September 19, 1864

**Pvt. Melzar Burton**  Killed in action at Gaines Mill, Virginia, June 27, 1862

**Pvt. Albert Churchill**  Missing, assumed killed while with Sheridan's scouts 1865

**Pvt. James Connor**  Killed in action at Morton's Ford, Virginia, November 27, 1863

**Corp. Benjamin Cummings**  Died of disease at Evansville, Indiana, August 1, 1862

**Pvt. Henry Dygert**  Killed in action at Gettysburg, Pennsylvania, July 2, 1863

**Farrier Pvt. John J. Ebbitt** Died of disease at Camp Dennison, Ohio, May, 1865

**Pvt. George W. Edgarton** Killed in action at Beaver Dam, Virginia, May 9, 1864

**Corporal George Ellsworth** Died of disease at Corinth, Mississippi, July 10, 1862

**Pvt. Charles Gass** Died of disease January 16, 1865

**Pvt. Charles T. Griffin** Died of disease at Nashville, Tennessee, January 24, 1863

**Pvt. Caleb F. Hall** Taken prisoner at Gettysburg, Pennsylvania and died March 3, 1864 of wounds

**Pvt. Sylvester Harvey** Wounded at Macon, Georgia and died in prison February 6, 1865

**Pvt. Justice Hedges** Wounded and died at Nashville, Tennessee, July 21, 1864

**Pvt. Andrew Hogan** Missing in action and later died at Andersonville Prison, Georgia, March 6, 1865

**Pvt. Samuel R. Howe** Taken prisoner, died in prison in Richmond, Virginia, November 1, 1863

**Pvt. Lanson Kinney** Died of disease March 27, 1864
**Corp. Joseph Mathews** Died of disease, September 8, 1863

**Pvt. Samuel L. Mathews** Wounded, later killed by Indians, Willow Springs, Colorado, July 13, 1865

**Pvt. Perry McConnell** Taken prisoner and died at Andersonville Prison, Georgia, January 1, 1865

**Pvt. Lafayette M. Reed**   Killed by accidental discharge of gun, September 1, 1864

**Pvt. John Reynolds**  Died in St. Mary's Hospital, Detroit. No further record.

**Pvt. Mica R. Rogers**  Wounded at Gaines Mill, Virginia and died in prison July 8, 1862

**Pvt. Charles Sitts**  Killed in action at Gettysburg, Pennsylvania, July 4, 1863

**Pvt. James Sumner**  Taken prisoner and died at Libby Prison, Richmond, Virginia, September 25, 1863

**Pvt. Charles H. Sutton**  Died of disease, New Market, Tennessee, March 30, 1865

**Pvt. James W. Travis**  Wounded, taken prisoner, died in prison at Richmond, Virginia, July 1862

**Pvt. Thomas H. Vandecar**   Taken prisoner, died later of wounds at Detroit, Michigan, May 26, 1865

**Pvt. Orrin Ward**  Taken prisoner and died in prison at Richmond, Virginia, December 31, 1863

**Pvt. Benedict Watson**  Died of disease at Chattanooga, Tennessee, October 21, 1864

**Corp. William H. Watson**   Killed in action at Buzzard's Roost, Georgia, February 25, 1864

**Pvt. Philip Wilcox, Jr.**   Killed in action at Gettysburg, Pennsylvania, July 3, 1863

# APPENDIX TWO

**Roster of Men who Answered the Call to Duty by Regiment**
(from the official Record of Service of Michigan Volunteers in the
Civil War 1861-1865)

## 1st Michigan Cavalry

Officers: Company L
**Captain, Melvin Brewer,** Almont. First Lieutenant, Hasbruck Reeve, Detroit. Second Lieutenant, John K. Truax, Grand Rapids.

**Armstrong, William,** Almont. Enlisted in Company L, First Cavalry, August 17, 1861, at Almont, for 3 years, age 22. Mustered Sept. 6, 1861. Deserted at Detroit, Mich., Sept. 7, 1861.

**Beach, Charles E.,** Almont. Enlisted in First Cavalry, Oct. 22, 1863, at Almont, for 3 years, age 25. Mustered Oct. 27, 1863. No further record.

**Black, Aretus E.,** Enlisted in company A, First Cavalry, as Corporal, Oct. 23, 1863, at Almont, for 3 years, age 25. Mustered Oct. 27, 1863. Promoted Sergeant June 1, 1865. Transferred to company E. Mustered out at Salt Lake City, Utah, March 10, 1866.

**Black, John S. or James,** Enlisted in Company B, First Cavalry, Feb. 23, 1864, at Almont, for 3 years, age 23. Mustered Feb. 27, 1864. Promoted Corporal. Discharged at Camp Douglas, Utah, Dec. 2, 1865.

**Brewer, Melvin,** Almont. Entered service in Company L, First Cavalry, at organization, as Captain. Aug. 9, 1861, at Almont, for

3 years, age 27. Commissioned Aug. 22, 1861. Mustered Sept. 6, 1861. Commissioned Major Jan. 1, 1863. Mustered Feb. 16, 1863. Wounded in action at Trevillian Station, Va., June 11, 1864. Commissioned Lieutenant Colonel, Seventh Cavalry, June 6, 1864. Not mustered. Died Sept. 25, 1864, of wounds received in action at Winchester, Va., Sept. 19, 1864.

**Churchill, Norvell F.,** Almont. Enlisted in Company L, First Cavalry, Aug.14, 1861, at Almont, for 3 years, age 21. Mustered Sept. 6, 1861. Discharged at expiration of term of service at Detroit, Mich., Feb. 25, 1865.

**Coleman, Richard B.,** Almont. Enlisted in Company L, First Cavalry, as Quartermaster Sergeant, Aug. 10, 1861, at Almont, for 3 years, age 38. Mustered Sept. 6, 1861. Discharged for disability July, 1862.

**Colerick, William,** Almont. Enlisted in Company L, First Cavalry, as First Sergeant, Aug. 17, 1861 at Almont, for 3 years, age 34. Mustered Sept. 6, 1861. Commissioned Second Lieutenant June 3, 1862. Transferred to Company I, May 18, 1863. Dismissed June 30, 1863. Re-entered service in Company L. Enlisted Aug. 23, 1864, at Pontiac, for 1 year. Mustered Aug. 23, 1864. Commissioned Captain, Company M, Dec. 4, 1864. Mustered Jan. 7, 1865. Acting Assistant Inspector General, First Brigade, First Cavalry Division, May and June, 1865. Transferred to Company F, Nov. 17, 1865. Mustered out at Fort Bridger, Utah, March 10, 1866

**Deneen, Edward H.,** Almont. Enlisted in Company L, First Cavalry, Aug. 10. 1861. at Almont, for 3 years, age 20. Mustered Sept. 6, 1861. Discharged at Stafford Court House by order of General Hooker.

**Deneen, John N.,** Almont. Enlisted in Company L, First Cavalry, as Corporal, Aug. 10, 1861, at Almont. for 3 years, age 44. Mustered Sept. 6, 1861. Re-enlisted Dec. 21, 1863. Mustered Dec. 21. 1863. Taken prisoner at Rappahannock River, Va. Paroled. Dishonorably discharged July 22, 1865.

**Edgerton, George W.**, Almont. Enlisted in Company L, First Cavalry, Oct. 6, 1862, at Almont, for 3 years, age 18. Mustered Oct. 20, 1862. Joined regiment at Harper's Ferry, Va., Dec. 22, 1862. Taken prisoner at Gettysburg, Pa., July 3, 1863. Returned to regiment at Culpepper, Va., Oct. 10, 1863. Killed in action at Beaver Dam, Va., May 9, 1864.

**Edgerton, or Edgeton, Joseph H.**, Almont. Enlisted in Company L, First Cavalry, Aug. 16, 1861, at Almont, for 3 years, age 24. Mustered Sept. 6, 1861. Re-enlisted Dec. 21, 1863. Mustered Dec. 21, 1863. Transferred to Company E, Nov. 17, 1865. Mustered out at Salt Lake City, Utah, March 10, 1866.

**Flannery, Michael**, Almont. Enlisted in Company L, First Cavalry, Aug. 20, 1861, at Almont, for 3 years, age 30. Mustered Sept. 6, 1861. Discharged Oct. 21, 1862, to enlist in the U. S. Army.

**French, Zadock K.**, Almont. Enlisted in Company L, First Cavalry, Aug. 14, 1861, at Almont, for 3 years, age 26. Mustered Sept. 6, 1861. Discharged at expiration of term of service Aug. 22, 1864.

**Guthrie, Phineas,** Enlisted in Company A, First Cavalry, as Corporal, Oct. 23, 1863, at Almont, for 3 years, age 21. Mustered Oct. 27, 1863. Transferred to Company E, Nov. 17, 1865. Mustered out at Salt Lake City, Utah, March 10, 1866.

**Hall, Caleb F.**, Almont. Enlisted in Company L, First Cavalry. Aug. 14, 1861, at Almont, for 3 years, age 26. Mustered Sept. 6, 1861. Taken prisoner at Gettysburg, Pa., July 3, 1863. Died March 3, 1864. Buried in National Cemetery at Marietta, Ga. Grave No. 6542.

**Hunt, James**, Almont. Enlisted in Company L, First Cavalry, Aug. 13, 1861, at Almont, for 3 years, age 27. Mustered Sept. 6, 1861. Deserted at Williamsport, Md., June 1, 1862.

**Irving, George W.**, Enlisted in Company A, First Cavalry, Oct. 23. 1863, at Almont, for 3 years, age 18. Mustered Oct. 27, 1863. Transferred to Company E, Nov. 17, 1865. Discharged at Fort Bridger, Utah, March 25, 1866.

**Ives, Edward H.**, Almont. Enlisted in Company L, First Cavalry, Aug. 14, 1861, at Almont, for 3 years, age 24. Mustered Sept. 6, 1861. Taken prisoner at Morton's Ford, VA., Nov. 27, 1863. Discharged Aug., 1865.

**Mathews, Samuel L.**, Enlisted in Company A, First Cavalry, Nov. 24, 1863, at Almont, for 3 years, age 18. Mustered Nov. 26, 1863. Entered Mower Hospital, Philadelphia, Pa., Sept. 21, 1864, on account of gunshot wound. Killed by Indians at Willow Springs, Colorado, Aug. 13, 1865.

**Ramsay, David,** Enlisted in Company A, First Cavalry, as Corporal, Oct. 25. 1863, at Almont, for 3 years, age 20. Mustered Oct. 27, 1863. Promoted First Sergeant Aug. 1, 1865. Transferred to Company E, Nov. 17, 1865. Mustered out at Salt Lake City, Utah, March 10, 1866.

**Rattray, John,** Almont. Enlisted in Company L. First Cavalry, as Sergeant, Aug. 10, 1861, at Almont, for 3 years, age 23. Mustered Sept. 6, 1861. Promoted First Sergeant July 1, 1862. Discharged at expiration of term of service Aug. 22, 1864.

**Reed, Darius**, Almont. Enlisted in Company L, First Cavalry, Aug. 14, 1861, at Almont, for 3 years, age 20. Mustered Sept. 6, 1861. Mustered out at expiration of term of service Aug. 22, 1864.

**Reed, Seymour,** Almont. Enlisted in Company L, First Cavalry, Aug. 13, 1861, at Almont, for 3 years, age 19. Mustered Sept. 6, 1861. Re-enlisted Feb. 5, 1864. Mustered Feb. 5, 1864. Taken prisoner at Shepardstown, VA., Aug. 25, 1864. Returned to regiment at Camp Stoneman, VA., Sept. 17, 1864. Discharged at Harper Hospital, Detroit, Mich., on account of wounds received in action.

**Remington, Alexander,** Enlisted in Company A, First Cavalry, Oct. 23, 1863, at Almont, for 3 years, age 26. Mustered in Oct. 27, 1863. No further record.

**Retherford, Lewis M.**, Enlisted in Company A, First Cavalry, as Corporal, Oct. 25, 1863, at Almont, for 3 years, age 22. Mustered in Oct. 27, 1863. Promoted First Sergeant. Transferred to Company B, Nov. 17, 1865. Promoted Commissary Sergeant. Mustered out at Salt Lake City, Utah, March 10, 1866.

**Russell, William,** Almont. Enlisted in Company L, First Cavalry, Aug. 17, 1861, at Almont, for 3 years, age 21. Mustered in Sept. 6, 1861. Re-enlisted Dec. 21, 1863. Mustered Dec. 21, 1863. Promoted Bugler. Taken prisoner at Winchester, VA., July 25, 1864. Discharged at Camp Chase, Ohio. June 7. 1865.

**Rutherford, William H.**, Almont. Enlisted in Company L, First Cavalry, as Corporal, Aug. 16, 1861, at Almont, for 3 years, age 27. Mustered Sept. 6. 1861. Re-enlisted Dec. 21, 1863. Mustered Dec. 21, 1863. Discharged at Salt Lake City, Utah, Nov. 30, 1865.

**Sands, James H.**, Almont. Enlisted in Company L, First Cavalry, Aug. 14, 1861, at Almont, for 3 years, age 22. Mustered Sept. 6, 1861. Deserted at Detroit, Mich., Sept. 16, 1861.

**Sheperd, Thomas H.**, Almont. Enlisted in Company L, First Cavalry, Aug. 20, 1861, at Almont, for 3 years, age 35. Mustered Sept. 6, 1861. Transferred to Company E, Jan., 1862. Taken prisoner at Gettysburg, Pa., July 3, 1863. Released at Venus Point, Ga., Nov. 18, 1864. Discharged at expiration of term of service March 28, 1865.

**Sheppard, Frederick G**. Enlisted in Company A, First Cavalry, Nov. 16, 1863, at Almont, for 3 years, age 17. Mustered Nov. 26, 1863. Discharged to date June 24, 1865.

**Sitts, Charles**, Almont. Enlisted in Company L, First Cavalry, Aug. 17, 1861, at Almont, for 3 years, age 18. Mustered in Sept. 6, 1861. Killed in action at Fairfield Gap, Md., July 4, 1863.

**Sitts, Orrin,** Enlisted in Company E, First Cavalry, Jan. 26, 1864, at Almont, for 3 years, age 18. Mustered Jan. 29, 1864. Discharged to date July 18, 1865.

**Steele or Stull, Peter,** Almont. Enlisted in Company L. First Cavalry, Aug., 1861, for 3 years. Mustered Sept. 17, 1861. Deserted at Sandy Hook, Md., Oct., 1862.

**Stringham, Owen W.,** Enlisted in Company A, First Cavalry, Oct. 23, 1863, at Almont, for 3 years, age 32. Mustered Oct. 27, 1863. Discharged at Philadelphia, Pa., May 19, 1865.

**Strobridge, William H.,** Almont. Enlisted in Company M, First Cavalry, Feb. 20, 1865, at Almont, for 1 year, age 17. Mustered March 4, 1865. Transferred to Company F, Nov. 17, 1865. Discharged at Fort Bridger, Utah, March 25, 1866.

**Taylor, Wallace W.,** Almont. Enlisted in Company L, First Cavalry, as Corporal, Aug. 16, 1861, at Almont, for 3 years, age 20. Mustered Sept. 6, 1861. Promoted Sergeant. Discharged at expiration of term of service Aug. 22, 1864.

**Vandecar, Thomas H.,** Enlisted in Company L, First Cavalry, Aug. 20, 1861, at Almont, for 3 years, age 19. Mustered Sept. 6, 1861. Taken prisoner at Robertson Run, VA., Sept. 23, 1863. Died at Detroit, Mich., May 26, 1865, of wounds received in action.

**Whalen, James,** Almont. Enlisted in Company L, First Cavalry, Aug. 16, 1861, at Almont, for 3 years, age 22. Mustered Sept. 6, 1861. Taken prisoner at Rappahannock River, VA., Aug. 20, 1862. Deserted at Annapolis, MD.

**Wilcox, Philip, Jr.,** Almont. Enlisted in Company L, First Cavalry, Aug. 14, 1861, at Almont, for 3 years, age 19. Mustered Sept. 6, 1861. Killed in action at Gettysburg, Pa., July 3, 1863.

**Wilkinson, John**, Almont. Enlisted in Company L, First Cavalry, Aug. 16, 1861, at Almont, for 3 years, age 21. Mustered in Sept. 6, 1861. Discharged for disability at Philadelphia, Pa., Jan. 13, 1863.

**Woodworth, Horace,** Almont. Enlisted in Company L, First Cavalry, Aug. 10, 1861, at Armada, for 3 years, age 18. Mustered Sept. 6, 1861. Re-enlisted Dec. 21, 1863. Mustered Dec. 21, 1863. Deserted at Fort Leavenworth, Kan.. July 1, 1865.

**Wright, Harrison L.**, Almont. Enlisted in Company L, First Cavalry, Feb. 26, 1862, at Detroit, for 3 years, age 21. Mustered in March 4, 1862. Re-enlisted Feb. 28, 1864, at Camp Stoneman, D. C., Mustered Feb. 29, 1864. Promoted to Corporal. Transferred to Company B, Dec. 9, 1864. Discharged at Detroit, Mich., Feb. 23, 1866.

## 2nd Michigan Cavalry

**Boynton, Michael**, Drafted for 3 years, from Almont, Lapeer County. Mustered in Nov. 23, 1863. Assigned to company B, Second Cavalry. Mustered out at Macon, Ga., Aug. 17, 1865.

**Jones, William,** Drafted for 3 years, from Almont, Lapeer County, age 18. Mustered Nov. 23, 1863. Assigned to company E, Second Cavalry. Mustered out at Macon, Ga., Aug. 17, 1865.

**McKay, Erastus D.,** Lapeer County. Enlisted in company H, Second Cavalry, as Farrier, Sept. 5, 1861, at Almont, for 3 years, age 33. Mustered in Oct. 2, 1861. Re-enlisted Jan. 5, 1864, at Mossy Creek, Tenn. Mustered March 29, 1864. Discharged at Jackson, Mich., Aug. 30, 1865.

**Turner, or Timmer, Henry**, Drafted for 3 years, from Almont, Lapeer County. Mustered Nov. 23, 1863. Assigned to company L, Second Cavalry. Transferred to Veteran Reserve Corps April 30, 1864.

**Braidwood, George S.,** Enlisted in company I, Third Cavalry, Sept. 4, 1863 at Almont, for 3 years, age 18. Mustered in Sept. 14, 1863. Joined regiment at Corinth, Miss., Oct. 18, 1863. Mustered out at San Antonio, Texas, Feb. 12, 1866.

**Marshall, Charles S.,** Enlisted in company I, Third Cavalry, Sept. 19. 1863, at Almont, for 3 years, age 18. Mustered in Sept. 19, 1863. Joined regiment at Corinth, Miss., Oct. 18, 1863. Mustered out at San Antonio, Texas, Feb. 12, 1866.

**Nowlin, George,** Enlisted in company K, Third Cavalry, Jan. 4, 1864, at Almont, for 3 years, age 19. Mustered in Jan. 9, 1864. Transferred to company H, June 9, 1865. Mustered out at San Antonio, Texas, Feb. 12, 1866.

**Nowlin, Michael,** Enlisted in Third Cavalry, Jan. 4, 1864, at Almont, for 3 years, age 23. Mustered in Jan. 9, 1864. No further record.

**Paton, William W.,** Enlisted in company I, Third Cavalry, Sept. 12, 1863, at Almont, for 3 years, age 18. Mustered in Sept. 12, 1863. Joined regiment at Corinth, Miss., Oct. 18, 1863. Mustered out at San Antonio, Texas, Feb. 12, 1866.

**Wallace, William.,** Enlisted in company I, Third Cavalry, Sept. 19, 1863, at Almont, for 3 years, age 18. Mustered in Sept. 19, 1863. Joined regiment at Corinth, Miss., Oct. 18, 1863. Transferred to company M, March 3, 1865. Mustered out at San Antonio, Texas, Feb. 12, 1866.

## 4th Michigan Cavalry

**Baird, Charles H.**, Almont. Enlisted in company A, Fourth Cavalry, Aug. 4, 1862, at Detroit, for 3 years, age 18. Mustered in Aug. 26, 1862. Bugler. Taken prisoner near Montgomery, Ala., April 11, 1865. Discharged at Detroit, Mich., July 21, 1865.

**Beach, Amos**, Almont. Enlisted in company G, Fourth Cavalry, Feb. 3, 1864, at Almont, for 3 years, age 44. Mustered in Feb. 5, 1864. Joined regiment at Nashville, Tenn., April 3, 1864. Died of disease at Columbia, Tenn., May 26, 1864. Buried in National Cemetery, Nashville, Tenn.

**Beach, Ansley B.**, Detroit. Enlisted in company D, Fourth Cavalry, Aug. 15, 1862, at Detroit, for 3 years, age 19. Mustered in Aug. 28, 1862. Corporal March 1, 1864. Wounded in action at Lovejoy, Ga., Aug. 15, 1864. Taken prisoner at Montgomery, Ala., March 13, 1865. Discharged at Detroit, Mich., July 21, 1865.

**Beach, Eady F.**, Almont. Enlisted in company A, Fourth Cavalry, Aug. 17, 1862, at Detroit, for 3 years, age 20. Mustered in Aug. 28, 1862. Died of disease at Bridgeport, Ala., Dec. 12, 1863. Buried in National Cemetery, Chattanooga, Tenn.

**Beach, George**, Enlisted in company G, Fourth Cavalry, Dec. 9, 1863, at Almont, for 3 years, age 17. Mustered in Dec. 10, 1863. Joined regiment at Nashville, Tenn., Feb. 28, 1864. Died of disease at Nashville, Tenn., Jan. 15, 1865. Buried in National Cemetery, Nashville, Tenn.

**Griffin, Charles T.**, Almont. Enlisted in company A, Fourth Cavalry, Aug. 1, 1862, at Detroit, for 3 years, age 44. Mustered in Aug. 28, 1862. Died of disease at Nashville, Tenn., Jan. 24, 1863. Buried in National Cemetery at Nashville, Tenn.

**Hogan, Andrew**, Almont. Enlisted in company A, Fourth Cavalry, July 29, 1862, at Detroit, for 3 years, age 25. Mustered in Aug. 28, 1862. Missing in action near Lovejoy's Station, Ga., Aug. 20, 1864. Died March 6, 1865. Buried in National Cemetery, Andersonville, Georgia.

**McCullough, Hiram**, Drafted for 3 years, from Almont, Lapeer County, age 25. Mustered in Dec. 2. 1863. Assigned to company I, Fourth Cavalry. Joined regiment at Nashville, Tenn., Feb. 28, 1864. Discharged at Edgefield, Tenn., Aug. 15, 1865.

## 5th Michigan Cavalry

**Churchill, Albert**, Almont. Enlisted in company A, Fifth Cavalry, Aug. 20, 1862, at Imlay City, for 3 years, age 21. Mustered Aug. 26, 1862. Missing since March 18, 1865. Supposed killed while with Sheridan's scouts.

**Churchill, John P.**, Almont. Enlisted in company A, Fifth Cavalry, Aug. 16, 1862, at Almont, for 3 years, age 29. Mustered Aug. 26, 1862. Promoted Corporal June 9, 1865. Mustered out at Fort Leavenworth, Kan., June 22, 1865.

**Connor, James,** Almont. Enlisted in company A, Fifth Cavalry, Aug. 16, 1862, at Almont, for 3 years, age 20. Mustered Aug. 26, 1862. Taken prisoner at Emmitsburg, Pa., July 4, 1863. Killed in action at Morton's Ford, Va., Nov. 27, 1863.

**Fitch, Lewis**, Almont. Enlisted in company A, Fifth Cavalry, Aug. 15, 1862, at Almont, for 3 years, age 18. Mustered in Aug. 28, 1862. Promoted Sergeant Jan. 1, 1865. Mustered out at Fort Leavenworth, Kan., June 22, 1865.

**Johnston, Benjamin F.**, Almont. Enlisted in company A, Fifth Cavalry, Aug. 16, 1862, at Bruce, for 3 years, age 33. Mustered in Aug. 26, 1862. Taken prisoner at Trevillian Station, Va., June 11, 1864. Honorably discharged at Detroit, Mich., July 10, 1865.

**Monroe, George L.**, Almont. Enlisted in company A, Fifth Cavalry, Aug. 16, 1862, at Bruce, for 3 years, age 21. Mustered in Aug. 26, 1862. Honorably discharged on Surgeon's certificate of disability Feb. 9, 1865.

**Phelps, Alexander**, Almont. Enlisted in company A, Fifth Cavalry, Aug. 20, 1862, at Pontiac, for 3 years, age 22. Mustered in Aug. 26, 1862. Deserted Oct. 22, 1862.

**Pierce, David**, Almont. Enlisted in company A, Fifth Cavalry, Aug. 15, 1862, at Almont, for 3 years, age 31. Mustered in Aug. 26, 1862. Taken prisoner at Emmitsburg, Pa., July 5, 1863. Paroled Aug. 5, 1863. Mustered out at Fort Leavenworth, Kan., June 22, 1865.

**Reynolds, John**, Almont. Enlisted in company A, Fifth Cavalry. Aug. 18, 1862, at Almont, for 3 years, age 24. Mustered in Aug. 26, 1862. Taken to St. Mary's Hospital, Detroit, Mich. No further record.

**Richmond, James**, Almont. Enlisted in company A, Fifth Cavalry, as Bugler, Aug. 18, 1862, at Almont, for 3 years, age 22. Mustered in Aug. 26, 1862. Mustered out at Fort Leavenworth, Kan., June 22, 1865.

**Stone, Addison R.**, Almont. Entered service in Fifth Cavalry, at organization, as Assistant Surgeon, age 34. Commissioned Sept. 25, 1862. Honorably discharged for disability Sept. 8, 1863.

**Sumner, James**, Almont. Enlisted in company A, Fifth Cavalry, Aug. 18, 1862, at Almont, for 3 years, age 35. Mustered in Aug. 26, 1862. Taken prisoner at Emmitsburg, Pa., July 4, 1863. Died in Libby prison, Richmond, Va., Sept. 25, 1863.

**Sutherland, Jerman**, Almont. Enlisted in company A, Fifth Cavalry, Aug. 16, 1862, at Almont, for 3 years, age 28. Mustered in Aug. 26, 1862, Taken prisoner near Richmond, Va., March 1, 1864. Returned to regiment May 20, 1865. Mustered out at Fort Leavenworth, Kan., June 22, 1865.

## *8ᵗʰ Michigan Cavalry*

Officers: Company E
Captain, **Andrew J. Abbey,** Romeo.
First Lieutenant,**Charles E. Greble**, Almont.
Second Lieutenant, **Robert F. Allen**, Plymouth.

**Amerman, Andrew V.**, Almont. Enlisted in company E, Eighth Cavalry, as First Sergeant, Nov. 11, 1862, at Almont, for 3 years, age 44. Mustered in Jan. 20, 1863. Discharged on Surgeon's certificate of disability at Pulaski, Tenn., June 4, 1865.

**Anderson, Joseph**, Enlisted in company E, Eighth Cavalry, Jan. 12, 1864, at Almont, for 3 years, age 18. Mustered in Jan. 22, 1864. Joined regiment at Mt. Sterling, Ky., Feb. 27, 1864. Died at Nashville, Tenn.,

**Babcock, Edward**, Almont. Enlisted in company E, Eighth Cavalry, Dec. 28. 1862, at Almont, for 3 years, age 29. Mustered in Jan. 20, 1863. Deserted at Covington, Ky., May 27, 1863.

**Babcock, Moses E.**, Almont. Enlisted in company L, Eighth Cavalry, March 16, 1863, at Almont, for 3 years, age 21. Mustered in April 23, 1863. No further record.

**Black, John S.**, Enlisted in company F, Eighth Cavalry, Feb. 23, 1864, at Almont, for 3 years, age 23. Mustered in Feb. 27, 1864. Joined regiment at Mt. Sterling, Ky., March 15, 1864. Mustered out at Nashville, Tenn., Sept. 22, 1865.

**Boles, A. N.**, Almont. Enlisted in company B, Eighth Cavalry, Dec. 30, 1862, at Almont, for 3 years, age 30. Mustered in Dec. 30, 1862. Deserted Dec. 9, 1864.

**Brooks, Robert**, Enlisted in unassigned, Eighth Cavalry, Jan. 19, 1864, at Almont, for 3 years, age 21. Mustered in Jan. 20, 1864. No further record.

**Burlingame, Merrick H.**, Almont. Enlisted in company E, Eighth Cavalry, as Farrier, Dec. 27, 1862, at Almont, for 3 years, age 38. Mustered in Jan. 20, 1863. Transferred to Veteran Reserve Corps, Aug. 10, 1864. Discharged at Elmira, N. Y., July 12, 1865, as Corporal of company K, Nineteenth Regiment, Veteran Reserve Corps.

**Burlison, Henry**, Almont. Enlisted in company E, Eighth Cavalry, Dec. 6, 1862, at Almont, for 3 years, age 18. Mustered in Jan. 20, 1863. Deserted July 28, 1863.

**Campbell, Thomas,** Enlisted in company E, Eighth Cavalry, Feb. 13, 1864, at Almont, for 3 years, age 23. Mustered in Feb. 15, 1864. Joined regiment at Mt. Sterling, Ky., March 10, 1864. Died of disease at Nashville, Tenn., Nov. 29, 1864. Buried at Nashville, Tenn.

**Clark, Isaac D. Jr.**, Almont. Enlisted in company E, Eighth Cavalry, as Saddler, Nov. 20, 1862, at Almont, for 3 years, age 21. Mustered in Jan. 20, 1863. Transferred to Invalid Corps Jan. 15, 1864. Discharged at Washington, D. C, July 27, 1865, from company K, Twelfth Regiment, Veteran Reserve Corps.

**Clark, Jacob,** Enlisted in company E, Eighth Cavalry, Jan. 4, 1864, at Almont, for 3 years, age 25. Mustered in Jan. 4, 1864. Joined regiment at Mt. Sterling, Ky., Feb. 27, 1864. Reported as of company L. Mustered out at Nashville, Tenn., Sept. 22, 1865.

**Clayton, Enoch**, Almont. Enlisted in company B, Eighth Cavalry, Dec. 25, 1862, at Lapeer, for 3 years, age 30. Mustered in Dec. 30, 1862. Transferred to company C. Deserted May 7, 1863.
**Cooley, Alvin,** Enlisted in company B, Eighth Cavalry, Dec. 23, 1862, at Almont, for 3 years, age 22. Mustered Dec. 30, 1862. Deserted Feb. 10, 1863.

**Croley, Cornelius D.**, Almont. Enlisted in company E, Eighth Cavalry, as Commissary Sergeant, Nov. 4, 1862, at Almont, for 3 years, age 23. Mustered in Jan. 20, 1863. Discharged to accept promotion, March 17, 1864. Commissioned Second Lieutenant,

Sept. 1, 1863. Mustered March 18, 1864. Commissioned First Lieutenant, Jan. 8, 1865. Resigned April 4, 1865.

**Crossit, William**, Almont. Enlisted in company L, Eighth Cavalry, March 15, 1863, at Almont, for 3 years, age 21. Mustered in April 23, 1863. Discharged at Camp Dennison, Ohio, Nov. 25, 1863.

**Downey, Edmund**, Enlisted in company E, Eighth Cavalry, Feb. 22, 1864, at Almont, for 3 years, age 45. Mustered in Feb. 27, 1864. Joined regiment at Mt. Sterling, Ky., March 10, 1864. Deserted at Camp Nelson, Ky., Sept. 29, 1864.

**Durkee, Phillip H.**, Almont. Enlisted in company E, Eighth Cavalry, Nov. 1, 1862, at Bloomfield, for 3 years, age 18. Mustered in Jan. 20, 1863. Deserted at Mt. Clemens, Mich., Jan. 27, 1863.

**Ebbitt, John J.**, Almont. Enlisted in company L, Eighth Cavalry, as Farrier, March 19, 1863, at Almont, for 3 years, age 21. Mustered in April 23, 1863. Died of disease at Camp Dennison, Ohio, May 1865.

**Gray, Frank**, Enlisted in unassigned, Eighth Cavalry, Dec. 28, 1863, at Almont, for 3 years, age 24. Mustered in Dec. 30, 1863. No further record.

**Greble, Charles E.**, Almont. Entered service in company E, Eighth Cavalry, as First Lieutenant, age 26. Commissioned Nov. 1, 1862. Mustered in Jan. 20, 1863. Commissioned Captain, Aug. 31, 1863. Mustered Nov. 21, 1863. Discharged at Pulaski, Tenn., July 20, 1865.

**Hall, James,** Enlisted in company F, Eighth Cavalry, Feb. 5, 1864, at Almont, for 3 years, age 18. Mustered in Feb. 9, 1864. Discharged for disability at Pulaski, Tenn., June 20, 1865.

**Hallack, John W.**, Enlisted in company E, Eighth Cavalry, Jan. 4, 1864, at Almont, for 3 years, age 19. Mustered in Jan. 4, 1864. Joined regiment at Mt. Sterling, Ky., Feb. 27, 1864. Reported as of company L. Mustered out at Nashville, Tenn., Sept. 22, 1865.

**Harvey, Coridon**, Enlisted in company E, Eighth Cavalry, Feb. 22, 1864, at Almont, for 3 years, age 35. Mustered in Feb. 27, 1864. Joined regiment at Mt. Sterling, Ky., March 10, 1864. Reported as of Company L. Mustered out at Nashville, Tenn., Sept. 22, 1865.

**Harvey, Henry**, Enlisted in company E, Eighth Cavalry, March 22, 1865, at Almont, for 1 year, age 26. Mustered in March 22, 1865. Joined regiment at Pulaski, Tenn., April 3, 1865. Reported as of company L. Mustered out at Nashville, Tenn., Sept. 22, 1865.

**Harvey, James S.**, Almont. Enlisted in company B, Eighth Cavalry, Dec. 21, 1862, at Almont, for 3 years, age 40. Mustered in Dec. 30, 1862. Transferred to company E. Discharged for disability at Detroit, Mich., June 30, 1863.

**Harvey, Stephen**, Almont. Enlisted in company E, Eighth Cavalry, Nov. 5, 1862, at Almont, for 3 years, age 30. Mustered in Jan. 20, 1863. Missing on raid to Macon, Ga., Aug. 4, 1864. Returned to regiment May 9, 1865. Reported as of company L. Mustered out at Nashville, Tenn., Sept. 22, 1865.

**Harvey, Sylvester**, Enlisted in company E, Eighth Cavalry, Jan. 25, 1864, at Almont, for 3 years, age 36. Mustered in Jan. 26, 1864. Joined regiment at Mt. Sterling, Ky., Feb. 27, 1864. Taken prisoner on raid to Macon, Ga., Aug. 4, 1864. Died in prison at Florence, S.C, Feb. 6, 1865.

**Hayes, John,** Enlisted in company L, Eighth Cavalry, Jan. 28, 1864, at Almont, for 3 years, age 40. Mustered in Jan. 28, 1864. Died of disease at Lexington, Ky., April 19, 1864. Buried in National Cemetery, Lexington, Ky.

**Hermance, Morgan,** Enlisted in company E, Eighth Cavalry, Jan. 28, 1864, at Almont, for 3 years, age 29. Mustered in Jan. 28, 1864. Deserted at Lexington, Ky., Sept. 20, 1864.

**Hill, Mitchell**, Enlisted in company E, Eighth Cavalry, Feb. 26, 1864, at Almont, for 3 years, age 24. Mustered in Feb. 27, 1864. Joined regiment at Camp Nelson, Ky., April 5, 1864. Reported as of company L. Mustered out at Nashville, Tenn., Sept. 22, 1865.

**Hilliker, Alfred**, Enlisted in company E, Eighth Cavalry, Jan. 13, 1864, at Almont, for 3 years, age 18. Mustered in Jan. 22, 1864. Joined regiment at Mt. Sterling, Ky., Feb. 27, 1864. Bugler. Missing on raid to Macon, Ga., Aug. 4, 1864. Returned to regiment Jan., 1865. Reported as of company L. Mustered out at Nashville, Tenn., Sept. 22, 1865.

**Hilliker, James**, Almont. Enlisted in company E, Eighth Cavalry, Dec. 29, 1862, at Almont, for 3 years, age 18. Mustered in Jan. 20, 1863. Missing on raid to Macon, Ga., Aug. 4, 1864. Returned to regiment May 12, 1865. Reported as of company L. Mustered out at Nashville, Tenn., Sept. 22, 1865.

**Hodson, Edwin R.**, Almont. Enlisted in company E, Eighth Cavalry, as Corporal Dec. 28, 1862, at Almont, for 3 years, age 26. Mustered in Jan. 20, 1863. Reported as of company L. Mustered out at Nashville, Tenn., Sept. 22, 1865.

**Howe, Lorenzo M.**, Almont. Enlisted in company E, Eighth Cavalry, Dec. 10, 1862, at Almont, for 3 years, age 19. Mustered in Jan. 20, 1863. Deserted at Mt. Clemens, Mich., March 20, 1863.

**Howe, Samuel R.**, Almont. Enlisted in company E, Eighth Cavalry, Dec. 26, 1862, at Almont, for 3 years, age 42. Mustered in Jan. 20, 1863. Taken prisoner at Athens, Tenn., Sept. 26, 1863. Died in prison at Richmond, Va., Nov. 1, 1863. Buried in National Cemetery at Richmond, Va.

**Hull, Mylon**, Almont. Enlisted in company E, Eighth Cavalry, Dec. 26, 1862. at Almont, for 3 years, age 26. Mustered in Jan. 20, 1863. Transferred to Invalid Corps, Jan. 15, 1864.

**Ives, Isaac**, Enlisted in company M, Eighth Cavalry, Jan. 19, 1864, at Almont, for 3 years, age 18. Mustered in Jan. 19, 1864. Joined regiment at Mt. Sterling, Ky., Feb. 27, 1864. Transferred to company F, July 20, 1865. Mustered out at Nashville, Tenn., Sept. 22, 1865.

**Klock, Alexander**, Enlisted in company E, Eighth Cavalry, May 25, 1864, at Almont, for 3 years, age 43. Mustered in Feb. 27, 1864. Joined regiment at Mt. Sterling, Ky., March 10, 1864. Reported as of company L. Mustered out at Nashville. Tenn., Sept. 22, 1865. .

**Loucks, Martin V.**, Almont. Enlisted in company B, Eighth Cavalry, Dec. 30, 1862, at Almont, for 3 years, age 27. Mustered in Dec. 30, 1862. Reported as of company G, Wagoner. Taken prisoner at Cleveland, Tenn., Sept. 18, 1863. Discharged at Nashville, Tenn., May 29, 1865.

**Mathews, Joseph**, Almont. Enlisted in company E, Eighth Cavalry, as Corporal, Dec. 27, 1862, at Almont, for 3 years, age 34. Mustered in Jan. 20, 1863. Died Sept. 8, 1863. Buried in "National Cemetery at Camp Nelson, Ky.

**Mathews, Veloris**, Almont. Enlisted in company E, Eighth Cavalry, Dec. 11, 1862, at Almont, for 3 years, age 19. Mustered in Jan. 20, 1863. Corporal Jan. 1, 1865. Reported as of company L. Mustered out at Nashville, Tenn., Sept. 22, 1865.

**McConnell, Perry**, Almont. Enlisted in company E, Eighth Cavalry, Dec. 22, 1862, at Almont, for 3 years, age 21. Mustered in Jan. 20, 1863. Taken prisoner on raid to Macon, Ga., Aug. 4, 1864. Died in prison at Andersonville, Ga., Jan. 1, 1865.

**McKee, Thomas W.**, Almont. Enlisted in company B, Eighth Cavalry, Dec. 30, 1862, at Almont, for 3 years, age 21. Mustered in Dec. 30, 1862. Reported as of company E, Oct., 1863. Corporal. Missing on raid to Macon, Ga., Aug. 4. 1864. Discharged at Detroit, Mich., June 9, 1865.

**McNall, Albertoss**, Almont. Enlisted in company G, Eighth Cavalry, Dec. 29, 1862. for 3 years, age 20. Mustered in Feb. 3, 1863. Deserted at Mt. Clemens, Mich., Feb. 5, 1863.

**McNall, Jeremiah**, Almont. Enlisted in company F, Eighth Cavalry, Dec. 11, 1862, at Almont, for 3 years, age 18. Mustered in Jan. 20, 1863. Transferred to company E. Deserted at Mt. Clemens, Mich., Feb. 20, 1863.

**Miles, George**, Almont. Enlisted in company B, Eighth Cavalry, Dec. 25, 1862, at Almont, for 3 years, age 22. Mustered in Dec. 30, 1862. Reported as of company E. Missing on raid to Macon, Ga., Aug. 4, 1864. Returned to regiment May 12, 1865. Discharged on Surgeon's certificate of disability at Pulaski, Tenn., June 30, 1865.

**Mills, Hubard**, Almont. Enlisted in company B, Eighth Cavalry, Dec. 28, 1862, at Almont, for 3 years, age 22. Mustered in Dec. 30, 1862. Deserted Feb. 15, 1863.

**Moon, Danford**, Almont. Enlisted in company E, Eighth Cavalry, Dec. 27, 1862, at Almont, for 3 years, age 31. Mustered in Jan. 20, 1863. Deserted at Mt. Clemens, Mich., Feb. 21, 1863:

**Nellison, William**, Almont. Enlisted in company E, Eighth Cavalry, Dec. 29, 1862, at Almont, for 3 years, age 26. Mustered in Jan. 20, 1863. Reported as of company L. Mustered out at Nashville, Tenn., Sept. 22, 1865.

**Nichols, Alvin**, Almont. Enlisted in company E, Eighth Cavalry, Dec. 22, 1862. at Almont, for 3 years, age 18. Mustered in Jan. 20, 1863. Deserted July 18, 1863.

**Nichols, Aura D.**, Almont. Enlisted in company E, Eighth Cavalry, as Sergeant, Dec. 22, 1862, at Almont, for 3 years, age 24. Mustered in Jan. 20. 1863. Reported as of company L, July, 1865. Mustered out at Nashville, Tenn., Sept. 22, 1865.

**Pratt, Ralph E.,** Almont. Enlisted in company E, Eighth Cavalry, Dec. 11, 1862, at Almont, for 3 years, age 21. Mustered in Jan. 20, 1863. Corporal, Jan. 1, 1865. Reported as of company L. Mustered out at Nashville, Tenn., Sept. 22, 1865.

**Riedel, Ernst,** Almont. Enlisted in company E, Eighth Cavalry, Dec. 26, 1862, at Almont, for 3 years, age 21. Mustered in Jan. 20, 1863. Transferred to Invalid Corps Jan. 15, 1864. Discharged June 17, 1865, from company F, Fifth Regiment, Veteran Reserve Corps.

**Rittenour, Henry,** Almont. Enlisted in company E, Eighth Cavalry, Dec. 29, 1862, at Almont, for 3 years, age 18. Mustered in Jan. 20, 1863. Deserted Feb. 10, 1863.

**Shellington, Frederick,** Almont. Enlisted in company E, Eighth Cavalry, Nov. 22, 1862, at Putnam, for 3 years, age 18. Mustered in Jan. 20, 1863. Missing on raid to Macon, Ga., Aug. 4, 1864. Discharged at Detroit, Mich., June 8, 1865.

**Sitts, Ezra,** Mayfield Township. Enlisted in company E, Eighth Cavalry, Feb. 25, 1864, at Almont, for 3 years, age 18. Mustered in Feb. 27, 1864. Joined regiment at Mt. Sterling, Ky., March 10, 1864. Reported as of company L. Mustered out at Nashville, Tenn., Sept. 22, 1865.

**Sitts, John,** Enlisted in company E, Eighth Cavalry, Feb. 25, 1864, at Almont, for 3 years, age 19. Mustered in Feb. 27, 1864. Joined regiment at Mt. Sterling, Ky., March 10, 1864. Reported as of company L. Mustered out at Nashville, Tenn., Sept. 22, 1865.

**Sitts, Morgan,** Enlisted in company E, Eighth Cavalry, Aug. 1, 1864, at Almont, for 3 years, age 25. Mustered Aug. 11, 1864. Substitute for Charles Kennute. Joined regiment at Pulaski, Tenn., May 9, 1865. Discharged at Detroit, Mich., June 16, 1865.

**Smith, Charles A.,** Enlisted in company E, Eighth Cavalry, Jan. 4, 1864, at Almont, for 3 years, age 20. Mustered in Jan. 4, 1864.

Joined regiment at Mt. Sterling, Ky., Feb. 27, 1864. Reported as of company L. Mustered out at Nashville, Tenn., Sept. 22, 1865.

**Taggart, Henry C.**, Almont. Enlisted in company E, Eighth Cavalry, Nov. 15, 1862, at Almont, for 3 years, age 21. Mustered in Jan. 20, 1863. Deserted at Mt. Clemens, Mich., March 20, 1863.

**Thomas, William**, Almont. Enlisted in company E, Eighth Cavalry, Nov. 18, 1862, at Almont, for 3 years, age 19. Mustered in Jan. 20, 1863. Reported as of company L. Mustered out at Nashville, Tenn., Sept. 22, 1865.

**Tompkins, Gillott**, Almont. Enlisted in company E, Eighth Cavalry, as Sergeant, Nov. 15, 1862, at Almont, for 3 years, age 22. Mustered in Jan. 20, 1863. Deserted at Mt. Clemens, Mich., March 28, 1863.

**Unger, Charles**, Almont. Enlisted in company H, Eighth Cavalry, Dec. 27, 1862, at Almont, for 3 years, age 26. Mustered in Feb. 3, 1863. Deserted at Mt. Clemens, Mich., May 27, 1863.

**VanDeusen, Mathew J.**, Almont. Enlisted in company E, Eighth Cavalry, Dec. 5. 1862, at Almont, for 3 years, age 30. Mustered in Jan. 20, 1863. Discharged for disability at Detroit, Mich., March 6, 1863.

**Wallace, Delavan D.**, Almont. Enlisted in company E, Eighth Cavalry, Dec. 29, 1862, at Almont, for 3 years, age 18. Mustered Jan. 20, 1863. Reported as of company L. Mustered out at Nashville, Tenn., Sept. 22, 1865.

**Ward, Charles H.**, Almont. Enlisted in company F, Eighth Cavalry, Dec. 20, 1862, at Almont, for 3 years, age 18. Mustered in Jan. 20, 1863. Reported as of company E, May, 1864. Taken prisoner on raid to Macon, Ga., Aug. 4, 1864. Confined at Andersonville, Ga., for 8 months. Discharged at Detroit, Mich., June, 1865.

**Ward, Orrin,** Almont. Enlisted in company E, Eighth Cavalry, Dec. 6, 1862, at Almont, for 3 years, age 19. Mustered in Jan. 20, 1863. Taken prisoner Nov. 24, 1863. Died in prison at Richmond, Va., Dec. 31, 1863. Buried in National Cemetery, Richmond, Va.

**Watson, Benedict**, Almont. Enlisted in company B, Eighth Cavalry, Dec. 28, 1862, at Almont, for 3 years, age 27. Mustered in Dec. 30, 1862. Reported in company E. Died at Chattanooga, Tenn., Oct. 21, 1864. Buried in National Cemetery, Chattanooga, Tenn.

**Watson, Eri**, Enlisted in company E, Eighth Cavalry, Feb. 25, 1864, at Almont, for 3 years, age 31. Mustered in Feb. 27, 1864. Joined regiment at Mt. Sterling, Ky., March 10, 1864. Reported as of company L. Mustered out at Nashville, Tenn., Sept. 22, 1865.

**Wells, Hiram C.,** Almont. Enlisted in company E, Eighth Cavalry, Nov. 10, 1862, as Quartermaster Sergeant, at Almont, for 3 years, age 37. Mustered in Jan. 20, 1863. Missing on raid to Macon, Ga., Aug. 4, 1864. Discharged at Detroit, Mich., June 9, 1865.

## 3rd Michigan Infantry

**Amsden, Charles,** Enlisted in company H, (reorganized) Third Infantry, Sept. 3, 1864, at Almont, for 3 years, age 18. Mustered in Sept. 7, 1864. Discharged at Benton Barracks, Mo., Sept. 26, 1865.

**Andrus, William R.,** Almont. Entered service in company H, Third Infantry, at reorganization as Captain. Commissioned July 29, 1864. Mustered in Sept. 23, 1864. Acting Assistant Inspector General Feb. 14, 1866. Commissioned Lieutenant Colonel Feb. 25, 1866. Mustered Feb. 26, 1866. Mustered out at Victoria, Texas, May 25, 1866.

**Black, Osmer D.,** Enlisted in company H, (reorganized) Third Infantry, Sept. 3, 1864, at Almont, for 3 years, age 32. Mustered in Sept. 7, 1864. Discharged at Detroit, Mich., April 24, 1866.

**Bowen, William,** Enlisted in company A, (reorganized) Third Infantry, Sept. 1, 1864, at Almont, for 3 years, age 33. Mustered in Sept. 7, 1864. Deserted at Pontiac. Mich., Oct. 19, 1864.

**Clark, James J.,** Enlisted in company H, (reorganized) Third Infantry, Aug. 29, 1864, at Almont, for 3 years, age 28. Mustered in Sept. 7, 1864. Discharged at Detroit, Mich., April 24, 1866.

**Crossman, James K.,** Enlisted in company H, (reorganized) Third Infantry, Oct. 4, 1864, at Almont, for 3 years, age 24. Mustered in Oct. 8, 1864. Mustered out at Victoria, Texas, May 25, 1866.

**Earity or Erity, Quail,** Enlisted in company H, (reorganized) Third Infantry, Aug. 31, 1864, at Almont, for 3 years, age 17. Mustered in Sept. 7, 1864. Mustered out at Victoria, Texas, May 25, 1866.

**Eaton, Orville B.,** Enlisted in company H, (reorganized) Third Infantry, Aug. 29, 1864, at Almont, for 3 years, age 18. Mustered in Sept. 7, 1864. Mustered out at Victoria, Texas, May 25, 1866.

**Fitch, Melvin J.,** Almont. Enlisted in company L., First Cavalry Aug. 15, 1861, at Almont, for 3 years, age 20. Mustered in Sept. 6, 1861. Discharged to accept promotion Oct. 20, 1862. Re-entered service. Enlisted in company H, (reorganized) Third Infantry, as Second Lieutenant. Commissioned July 29, 1864. Mustered Sept. 23. 1864. Transferred to company K, March, 1865. Commissioned First Lieutenant, company C. March 12, 1865. Mustered April 22, 1865. Resigned on account of disability. June 30, 1865.

**Goodsell, Harmon G.,** Enlisted in company H, (reorganized) Third Infantry, Oct. 6, 1864, at Almont, for 3 years, age 23. Mustered in Oct. 8, 1864. Deserted at Cairo, Ill., June 19, 1865.

**Grant, James,** Enlisted in company H, (reorganized) Third Infantry, Oct. 3, 1864, at Almont, for 3 years, age.44. Mustered in Oct. 8, 1864. Deserted at Pontiac, Mich., Oct. 19, 1864.

**Gregory, Melvin,** Enlisted in company H, (reorganized) Third Infantry, Sept. 3, 1865, at Almont, for 3 years, age 35. Mustered in Sept. 8, 1864. Discharged at Detroit, Mich., May 27, 1865.

**Hall, Eton J.,** Enlisted in company H, (reorganized) Third Infantry, Oct. 7, 1864, at Almont, for 3 years, age 18. Mustered in Oct. 8, 1864. Discharged at Detroit, Mich., April 13, 1866.

**Hamilton, Michael J.,** Enlisted in company H, (reorganized) Third Infantry, Sept. 3, 1864, at Almont, for 3 years, age 33. Mustered in Sept. 7, 1864. Admitted to Harper Hospital Sept. 16, 1865. Discharged at Detroit, Mich., Sept. 26, 1865.

**Hathaway, Erastus,** Enlisted in company H, (reorganized) Third Infantry, Sept. 3, 1864 at Almont, for 3 years, age 25. Mustered in Sept. 7, 1864. Mustered out at Victoria. Texas, May 25, 1866.

**Helmka, Thomas,** Enlisted in company H, (reorganized) Third Infantry, Sept. 3, 1864, at Almont, for 3 years, age 19. Mustered in Sept. 7, 1864. Mustered out at Victoria, Texas, May 25, 1866.

**Horan, Patrick,** Enlisted in company H, (reorganized) Third Infantry, Aug. 13, 1864, at Almont, for 3 years, age 18. Mustered in Sept. 7, 1864. Discharged at St. Louis, Mo., March 20, 1865.

**Hull, Henry,** Enlisted in company H, (reorganized) Third Infantry, Aug. 29, 1864, at Almont, far 3 years, age 19. Mustered in Sept. 7, 1864. Mustered out at Victoria, Texas, May 25, 1866.

**King, Daniel D.,** Enlisted in company H, (reorganized) Third Infantry, Sept. 1, 1864, at Almont, for 3 years, age 30. Mustered in Sept. 7, 1864. Musician Nov., 1864. Discharged at Detroit, Mich., April 24, 1866.

**King, Marcus E.,** Enlisted in company H, (reorganized) Third Infantry, Aug. 31, 1864, at Almont, for 3 years, age 17. Mustered in Sept. 7, 1864. Discharged at Knoxville, Tenn., May 22, 1865. .

**Lawrence, Francis,** Enlisted in company H, (reorganized) Third Infantry, Aug. 31, 1864, at Almont, for 3 years, age 22. Mustered in Sept., 1864. Deserted at Pontiac, Mich., Oct. 19, 1864.

**Lawrence, William L.,** Enlisted in company H (reorganized) Third Infantry, Aug. 31, 1864, at Almont, for 3 years, age 42. Mustered in Sept. 7, 1864. Admitted to Harper Hospital June 27, 1865. Discharged at Detroit, Mich., Sept. 18, 1865.

**Murdock, John,** Enlisted in company H, (reorganized) Third Infantry, Sept. 3, 1864, at Almont, for 3 years, age 44. Mustered in Sept. 8. 1864. Mustered out at Victoria, Texas, May 25, 1866.

**Murdock, William,** Enlisted in company H, (reorganized) Third Infantry, Sept. 3, 1864, at Almont, for 3 years, age 18. Mustered in Sept. 7, 1864. Mustered out at Victoria, Texas, May 25, 1866.

**Rood, Robert S.,** Enlisted in company H, (reorganized) Third Infantry, as Corporal, Aug. 29, 1864, at Almont, for 3 years, age 30. Mustered in Sept. 7, 1864. Corporal Sept. 23, 1864. Sick at Nashville, Tenn., Nov. 24, 1864.

**Ross, Charles E.,** Enlisted in company H, (reorganized) Third Infantry, Aug. 31, 1864, at Almont, for 3 years, age 21. Mustered in Sept. 7, 1864. Admitted to Harper Hospital April 27, 1865. Discharged at Detroit, Mich., May, 1865.

**Ross, David P.,** Enlisted in company H, (reorganized) Third Infantry, Aug. 31, 1864, at Almont, for 3 years, age 28. Mustered in Sept. 7, 1864. Admitted to Harper Hospital June 27, 1865. Discharged at Detroit, Mich., Sept. 18, 1865.

**Sutton, Charles H.,** Enlisted in company H, (reorganized) Third Infantry, Sept. 3, 1864, at Almont, for 3 years, age 19. Mustered Sept. 7, 1864. Died at New Market, Tenn., March 30, 1865. Buried in National Cemetery, Knoxville, Tenn.

**Wilcox, Erastus W.,** Enlisted in company H, (reorganized) Third Infantry, Sept. 3, 1864 at Almont, for 3 years, age 37. Mustered in Sept. 7, 1864. Mustered out at Victoria, Texas, May 25, 1866.

**Winn, Peter,** Enlisted in company H, (reorganized) Third Infantry, Aug. 31, 1864, at Almont, for 3 years, age 25. Mustered in Sept. 7, 1864. Admitted to Harper Hospital Aug. 6, 1865. Discharged at Detroit, Mich. Sept., 1865.

**James, George K....**no record

**Wheelock, Granville...**no record

## *10ᵗʰ Michigan Infantry*

Officers: **Company F**
Captain, **Walter P. Beach**, Lapeer.
First Lieutenant, **Noah H. Hart**, Lapeer.
Second Lieutenant, **Calvin M. Hall,** Almont.

**Armstrong, William**, Almont. Enlisted in company F, Tenth Infantry, Nov. 2, 1861, at Almont, for 3 years, age 20. Mustered in Feb. 6, 1862. Discharged for disability at Detroit, Mich., July 17, 1862.

**Atwell, Ogden**, Almont. Enlisted in company F, Tenth Infantry, Feb. 27, 1864, at Dryden, for 3 years, age 27. Mustered in Feb. 29, 1864. Mustered out at Louisville, Ky., July 19, 1865.

**Becraft, John Edmund**, Almont. Enlisted in company F, Tenth Infantry, Feb. 16, 1862, at Lapeer. Mustered in May 1, 1862. Taken prisoner and paroled Aug. 9, 1862. Discharged for disability at Detroit, Mich., June 15, 1863.

**Bradley, Andrew W.,** Enlisted in company F, Tenth Infantry, as Corporal, Dec. 20, 1861, at Almont, for 3 years, age 32. Mustered in Feb. 6, 1862. Re-enlisted Feb. 6, 1864, at Rossville, Ga. Mustered Feb. 16, 1864. Wounded at Peach Tree Creek, Ga., July 20, 1864. Sergeant. Discharged for disability at Jeffersonville, Ind., July 13, 1865. Gun shot wound.

**Burton, Norman,** Enlisted in company F, Tenth Infantry, Nov. 25, 1861, at Almont, for 3 years, age 18. Mustered in Feb. 6, 1862. Re-enlisted Feb. 6, 1864, at Rossville, Ga. Mustered Feb. 16, 1864. Mustered out at Louisville, Ky., July 19, 1865.

**Clark, Levi C.**, Almont. Enlisted in company F, Tenth Infantry, Feb. 29, 1864 at Pontiac, for 3 years, age 38. Mustered in Feb. 29, 1864. Mustered out at Louisville, Ky., July 19, 1865.

**Cummings, Benjamin**, Enlisted in company F, Tenth Infantry, as Corporal, Dec. 23, 1862, at Almont, for 3 years, age 23. Mustered in Feb. 6. 1862. Died of disease at Evansville, Ind., Aug. 1, 1862. Buried at Evansville, Ind.

**Ellsworth, Charles,** Almont. Enlisted in company G, Tenth Infantry, Dec. 17, 1861, at Almont, for 3 years, age 21. Mustered in Feb. 6, 1862. Re-enlisted Feb. 6, 1864, at Rossville, Ga. Mustered Feb. 16, 1864. Sergeant. Mustered out at Louisville, Ky., July 19, 1865.

**Ferguson, James A.,** Almont. Enlisted in company F, Tenth Infantry, Nov. 25, 1861, at Almont, for 3 years, age 19. Mustered in Feb. 6, 1862. Re-enlisted Feb. 6, 1864, at Rossville, Ga., Mustered Feb. 16, 1864. Wounded Feb. 1864. Corporal May 1, 1865. Mustered out at Louisville, Ky., July 19, 1865.

**Fisher, Linus G.**, Almont. Enlisted in company F, Tenth Infantry. Jan. 5, 1862, at Almont, for 3 years, age 25. Mustered in Feb. 6, 1862. Discharged for disability at Detroit, Mich., July 22, 1862.

**Fisher, Warren**, Almont. Enlisted in company F, Tenth Infantry, Nov.15, 1861 at Almont, for 3 years, age 38. Mustered in Feb. 6. 1862. Re-enlisted Feb. 6, 1864 at Rossville, Ga. Mustered Feb. 16, 1864. Mustered out at Louisville, Ky., July 19, 1865.

**Glover, William M.,** Almont. Enlisted in company F, Tenth Infantry, Nov. 2, 1861, at Almont, for 3 years, age 38. Mustered in Nov. 2, 1861. Re-enlisted Feb. 6, 1864 at Rossville, Ga. Mustered in Feb. 16. 1864. Mustered out at Louisville, Ky., July 19, 1865.

**Hall, Calvin M.,** Almont. Entered service in company F. Tenth Infantry, at organization, as Second Lieutenant, Oct. 25, 1861, at Almont, for 3 years, age 32. Commissioned to date Oct. 1, 1861, Mustered in Feb. 6, 1862. Resigned and honorably discharged June 2, 1862.

**Hedges, Justice,** Almont. Enlisted in company G, Tenth Infantry, Dec. 12, 1861, for 3 years, age 18. Mustered in Feb. 6, 1862. Re-enlisted Feb. 6, 1864, at Rossville, Ga. Mustered Feb. 16. 1864. Died at Nashville, Tenn., Aug. 30, 1864 of wounds received in action at Peach Tree Creek, Ga., July 21, 1864. Buried in National Cemetery at Nashville, Tenn.

**Hodgson, James O.,** Almont. Enlisted in company F, Tenth Infantry, Feb. 20, 1862, at Lapeer, for 3 years, age 23. Mustered in Feb. 20, 1862. Re-enlisted Feb. 20, 1864, at Rossville, Ga. Mustered March 22, 1864. Mustered out at Louisville, Ky., July 19, 1864.

**Lenox, Marvin,** Almont. Enlisted in company G, Tenth Infantry, Oct. 15, 1861, at Lapeer, for 3 years, age 21. Mustered in Feb. 6, 1862. Re-enlisted Feb. 6, 1864, at Rossville. Ga. Mustered Feb. 16, 1864. Corporal June, 1865. Mustered out at Louisville, K., July 19, 1865.

**McMonegal, Cornelius,** Almont. Enlisted in company F, Tenth Infantry, Nov. 2, 1861, at Almont, for 3 years, age 39. Mustered in Feb. 2, 1862. Re-enlisted Feb. 2, 1864, at Rossville, Ga. Mustered Feb. 16, 1864. Wounded in action Sept. 1, 1864. Corporal June, 1865. Mustered out at Louisville, Ky., July 19, 1865.

**Middleditch, Albert,** Almont. Enlisted in company F, Tenth Infantry, Nov. 26. 1861, at Almont, for 3 years, age 20. Mustered in Feb. 6, 1862. Discharged for disability at Detroit, Mich., July 4, 1862.

**Miller, Clinton.** Enlisted in company F, Tenth Infantry, Feb. 22, 1862, at Almont, for 3 years, age 19. In Engineer's Corps from Nov. 1862 to Feb., 1865. Discharged at expiration of term of service Feb. 27, 1865.

**Nolin, Owen,** Almont. Enlisted in company F, Tenth Infantry, Jan. 23, 1862, at Almont, for 3 years, age 23. Mustered in Feb. 6, 1862, Re-enlisted Feb. 6, 1864, at Rossville, Ga. Mustered Feb. 16, 1864. Corporal May 1, 1865. Mustered out at Louisville, Ky., July 19, 1865.

**Owen, Tallman C.** (Veteran), Almont. Enlisted in company F, Tenth Infantry, Jan. 23, 1862, at Almont, for 3 years, age 20. Mustered in Jan. 23, 1862. Re-enlisted Feb. 6, 1864, at Rossville, Ga. Mustered Feb. 16, 1864. Wounded at Peach Tree Creek, Ga., July 20, 1864. Mustered out at Louisville, Ky., July 19, 1865.

**Reed, Darwin,** Almont. Enlisted in company F, Tenth Infantry, Nov. 25, 1861, at Almont, for 3 years, age 22. Mustered in Feb. 6, 1862. Re-enlisted Feb. 6, 1864. at Rossville, Ga. Mustered Feb. 16, 1864. Corporal May 1, 1865. Mustered out at Louisville, Ky., July 19, 1865.

**Reed, Lafayette M.**, Almont. Enlisted in company F, Tenth Infantry, Nov. 18, 1861, at Almont, for 3 years, age 29. Mustered in Feb. 6, 1862. Re-enlisted Feb. 6, 1864, at Rossville, Ga. Mustered Feb. 16, 1864. Killed by accidental discharge of gun near Jonesboro, Ga., Sept. 1, 1864.

**Reed, William A.**, Almont. Enlisted in company F, Tenth Infantry, Nov. 13, 1861, at Almont, for 3 years, age 30. Mustered in Feb. 6, 1862. Discharged for disability at Detroit, Mich. July 12, 1862.

**Roberts, Ami M.**, Almont. Enlisted in company F, Tenth Infantry, as Bugler. Dec. 25, 1861, at Almont, for 3 years, age 25. Mustered in Feb. 6, 1862. Re-enlisted as Quartermaster Sergeant, Feb. 6, 1864, at Rossville, Ga. Mustered Feb. 16, 1864. Discharged to accept promotion March 26, 1865. Commissioned First Lieutenant and Quartermaster Dec. 31, 1864. Mustered March 27, 1865. Mustered out at Louisville, Ky., July 19, 1865.

**Stevens, Calvin,** Almont. Enlisted in company F, Tenth Infantry, Jan. 27, 1862, for 3 years. Mustered in Feb. 6, 1862. Discharged for disability at Detroit, Mich., Sept. 30, 1862.

**Watson, William H.**, Enlisted in company F, Tenth Infantry, Nov. 8, 1861, at Almont, for 3 years, age 18. Mustered in Nov. 8, 1861. Corporal. Killed in action at Buzzard's Roost, Ga., Feb. 25, 1864.

## *15ᵗʰ Michigan Infantry*

**Ellsworth, George**, Almont. Enlisted in company E, Fifteenth Infantry, as Corporal, Oct. 29, 1861, at Almont, for 3 years, age 19. Mustered in Jan. 29, 1862. In battle of Shiloh. Tenn. Died of disease at Corinth, Miss., July 10, 1862.

# 16th Michigan Infantry

**Burton, Melzar** see Dygert's Sharpshooters

**Cedar, Cater, or Kator, Calvin**, Almont. Enlisted in company K. Sixteenth Infantry, Feb. 5, 1862, at Almont, for 3 years, age 23. Mustered in March 24, 1862. Reported as of company H. Dropped from rolls Aug. 7, 1863.

**Dygert, Henry**, Almont. Enlisted in company K, Sixteenth Infantry, Feb. 5, 1862, at Almont, for 3 years, age 24. Mustered in March 24, 1862. Transferred to company B. Killed in action at Gettysburg, July 2, 1863

**Gilbert, George B.**, Almont. Enlisted in company K, Sixteenth Infantry, Feb. 5. 1862, at Almont, for 3 years, age 38. Mustered in March 24, 1862. Transferred to company D. Discharged at Fortress Monroe, Va., Sept. 21, 1862.

**Haggadone, William**, Almont. Enlisted in company K, Sixteenth Infantry, Feb. 5, 1862, at Almont, for 3 years, age 35. Mustered in March 24, 1862. Transferred to company D. Discharged at Philadelphia, Pa., Jan. 11, 1863, on account of wounds received in action at Gaines Mill, Va., June 27, 1862.

**Lyons, John**, Almont. Enlisted in company K, Sixteenth Infantry, Feb, 5, 1862, at Almont, for 3 years, age 35. Mustered in March 24. 1862.

**Mathews, Theodore**, Almont. Enlisted in company K, Sixteenth, Infantry, Feb. 5, 1862, at Almont, for 3 years, age 20. Mustered in March 24, 1862. Transferred to company H. Re-enlisted Dec. 27, 1863, at Rappahannock Station, Va. Mustered Dec. 28, 1863. Wounded in action June 19, 1864. No further record.

**Maxon, W.**, Almont. Enlisted in company K, Sixteenth Infantry, Feb. 5, 1862, at Almont, for 3 years, age 40. Mustered in March 24, 1862. Transferred to company E. No further record.

**Rogers, Mica** see Dygert's Sharpshooters

**Travis, James W.**, Enlisted in company K, Sixteenth Infantry, Feb. 5. 1862, at Almont, for 3 years, age 22. Mustered in March 24, 1862. Transferred to company D. Joined regiment at Hall's Hill, Va., Feb. 14, 1862. Wounded and taken prisoner at Gaines' Mills, Va., June 27, 1862. Died in prison at Richmond, Va., July, 1862.

## *Dygert's sharpshooters, 16th Michigan Infantry*

**Burton, Melzar**, Almont. Enlisted in First Company Sharpshooters, attached to Sixteenth Infantry, Nov. 14, 1861, at Detroit, for 3 years, age 20. Mustered in Jan. 23, 1862. Joined regiment at Mall's Hill, Va., Feb. 14, 1862. Killed in action at Gaines Mill, Va., June 27, 1862.

**Rogers, Mica R.**, Almont. Enlisted in First Company Sharpshooters, attached to Sixteenth Infantry, Dec. 18, 1861, at Detroit, for 3 years, age 39. Mustered in Dec. 18, 1861. Wounded and taken prisoner at Gaines Mill, Va., June 27, 1862. Died in prison at Richmond, Va., July 8, 1862, of wounds received in action at Gaines Mill, Va., June 27, 1862.

## *22ⁿᵈ Michigan Infantry*

**Fox, Alexander E.**, Enlisted in company D, Twenty-second Infantry, Feb. 13, 1864, at Almont, for 3 years, age 29. Mustered in Feb. 13, 1864. Joined regiment at Chattanooga, Tenn., March 22, 1864. Transferred to company D, Twenty-ninth Infantry, June 26, 1865. Mustered out at Murfreesboro, Tenn., Sept. 6. 1865.

**Hamilton, William B.**, Almont. Enlisted in company B. Twenty-second Infantry, as Sergeant, Aug. 8, 1862, at Romeo, for 3 years, age 32. Mustered in Aug. 14, 1862. Discharged to accept promotion June 29, 1863. Commissioned Second Lieutenant, company F, to date June 5, 1863. Mustered June 29, 1863. Taken prisoner at Chickamauga, Ga., Sept. 20, 1863. Paroled March 1, 1865. Returned to regiment May 9, 1865. Commissioned First Lieutenant to date Nov. 17, 1863. Mustered to date July 30, 1864. Mustered out at Nashville, Tenn., June 26, 1865.

**Kenny, or Kinney, Lanson**, Enlisted in unassigned, Twenty-second Infantry, Feb. 27, 1864, at Almont, for 3 years, age 19. Mustered in March 5, 1864. Died of disease, March 27, 1864.

**Paton, David**, Almont. Enlisted in company B, Twenty-second Infantry, Aug. 9, 1862, at Romeo, for 3 years, age 23. Mustered in Aug. 14, 1862. Transferred to U. S. Signal Corps Oct. 18, 1863. Discharged at St. Louis, Mo., July 10. 1865.

**Paton, John H.**, Almont. Enlisted in company B, Twenty-second Infantry, Aug. 9, 1862, at Romeo, for 3 years, age 19. Mustered in Aug. 14, 1862. Corporal April, 1863. Transferred to U. S. Signal Corps Oct. 28, 1863. Discharged at St. Louis, Mo., July 10, 1865.

**Fechting, Andrew,** Almont. Enlisted in company H, Twenty-fourth Infantry, March 2. 1865. at Pine River, for 1 year, age 42. Mustered in March 7, 1865. Joined regiment at Springfleld, Ill., March 17, 1865. Mustered out at Detroit, Mich., June 30, 1865.

### *30ᵗʰ Michigan Infantry*

**Apling, Charles F.,** Enlisted in company B, Thirtieth Infantry, Dec. 9, 1864, at Almont, for 1 year, age 30. Mustered in Dec. 13, 1864. Corporal Dec. 24, 1864. Mustered out at Detroit, Mich., June 30, 1865.

**Banister, Lucien,** Enlisted in company D, Thirtieth Infantry, Dec. 20, 1864, at Almont, for 1 year, age 20. Mustered in Dec. 30, 1864. Mustered out at Detroit, Mich., June 30, 1865.

**Bentley, James J.,** Enlisted in company B, Thirtieth Infantry, Dec. 5, 1864, at Almont, for 1 year, age 35. Mustered in Dec. 13, 1864. Mustered out at Detroit, Mich., June 30, 1865.

**Bowen, George,** Enlisted in company I). Thirtieth Infantry, Dec. 17, 1864, at Almont, for 1 year, age 21. Mustered in Dec. 30, 1864. Mustered out at Detroit, Mich., June 30, 1865.

**Churchill, Charles,** Enlisted in company I, Thirtieth Infantry, Dec. 13, 1864, at Almont, for 1 year, age 21. Mustered in Dec. 13, 1864, Mustered out at Detroit, Mich., June 30, 1865.

**Coleman, Legrand M.,** Enlisted in company B. Thirtieth Infantry, Dec. 10, 1864 at Almont, for 1 year, age 19. Mustered in Dec. 15, 1864. Mustered out at Detroit, Mich., June 30, 1865.

**Davis, Homer,** Enlisted in company B. Thirtieth Infantry, Dec. 8, 1864, at Almont, for 1 year, age 35. Mustered in Dec. 13, 1864, Corporal Dec. 24. 1864, Mustered out at Detroit, Mich., June 30, 1865.

**Dewey, Orange,** Enlisted in company B, Thirtieth Infantry, Dec. 13, 1864. at Almont, for 1 year, age 20. Mustered in Dec. 15, 1864. Mustered out at Detroit, Mich., June 30, 1865.

**Dickinson, Leonidas**, Enlisted in company B. Thirtieth Infantry, Dec. 15. 1864, at Almont, for 1 year, age 26. Mustered in Dec. 15, 1864. Corporal Dec. 24, 1864. Mustered out at Detroit, Mich., June 30, 1865.

**Eaton, Collins D.**, Enlisted in company B, Thirtieth Infantry, Dec. 15, 1864. at Almont, for 1 year, age 30. Mustered in Dec. 15, 1864. Mustered out at Detroit, Mich., June 30, 1865.

**Fox, Lowell**, Almont. Enlisted in company D, Thirtieth Infantry, Dec. 19. 1864, at Almont, for 1 year, age 17. Mustered in Dec. 30, 1864. Mustered out at Detroit, Mich., June 30, 1865.

**Fox, Milton**, Enlisted in company B, Thirtieth Infantry, Dec. 3. 1864, at Almont, for 1 year, age 19. Mustered in Dec. 15, 1864. Mustered out at Detroit, Mich., June 30, 1865.

**Fox, Sylvester**, Enlisted in company D, Thirtieth Infantry, Dec. 19, 1864, at Almont, for 1 year, age 39. Mustered in Dec. 30, 1864. Mustered out at Detroit, Mich., June 30, 1865.

**Gass, Charles**, Enlisted in company I, Thirtieth Infantry, Dec. 6. 1864, at Almont, for 1 year, age 32. Mustered in Dec. 13, 1864, Died of disease, Jan. 16, 1865.

**Gass, Homer**, Enlisted in company B, Thirtieth Infantry, Dec. 6, 1804, at Almont, for 1 year, age 22. Mustered in Dec. 13, 1864. Mustered out at Detroit, Mich., June 30, 1865.

**Gass, John W.**, Enlisted in company B, Thirtieth Infantry, Dec. 6, 1864, at Almont, for 1 year, age 18. Mustered in Dec. 13, 1864 Musician. Mustered out at Detroit, Mich., June 30, 1865.

**Humphrey, Alonzo A.**, Enlisted in company D. Thirtieth Infantry, Dec. 22, 1864, at Almont, for 1 year, age 19. Mustered in Dec. 30, 1864. Mustered out at Detroit, Mich., June 30, 1865.

**Lyon, Munson E.**, Enlisted in company B, Thirtieth Infantry, Dec. 5, 1864 at Almont, for 1 year, age 24. Mustered in Dec. 13, 1864. Corporal Dec. 24, 1864. Mustered out at Detroit, Mich., June 30, 1865.

**McCollough, Birdseye**, Enlisted in company B, Thirtieth Infantry, Dec. 10, 1864, at Almont, for 1 year, age 17. Mustered in Dec. 13, 1864. Mustered, out at Detroit, Mich., June 30, 1865.

**McRoy or McRay, William C.**, Enlisted in company D, Thirtieth Infantry, Dec. 14, 1864, at Almont, for 1 year, age 20. Mustered in Dec. 30, 1864. Mustered out at Detroit, Mich., June 30, 1865.

**Norton, Byron**, Enlisted in company B, Thirtieth Infantry, Dec. 6, 1864, at Almont, for 1 year, age 31. Mustered in Dec. 15, 1864, musician Jan., 1865. Mustered out at Detroit, Mich., June 30, 1865.

**Potter, Lewis**, Enlisted in company B, Thirtieth Infantry, Dec. 14, 1864 at Almont, for 1 year, age 35. Mustered in Dec. 15, 1864. Corporal Dec. 24, 1864. Mustered out at Detroit, Mich., June 30, 1865.

**Robinson, Rodney D.**, Enlisted in company B, Thirtieth Infantry, Dec. 8, 1864, at Almont, for 1 year, age 22. Mustered in Dec. 13, 1864. Corporal Dec. 24, 1864. Mustered out at Detroit, Mich., June 30, 1865.

**Ross, William**, Enlisted in company D, Thirtieth Infantry, Dec. 28, 1864, at Almont, for 1 year, age 18. Mustered in Dec. 30, 1864. Mustered out at Detroit, Mich., June 30, 1865.

**Snover, Albert S.**, Enlisted in company B, Thirtieth Infantry, Dec. 7, 1864. at Almont, for 1 year, age 26. Mustered in Dec. 13, 1864. Mustered out at Detroit, Mich., June 30, 1865.

**Snover, Ozias,** Enlisted in company D, Thirtieth Infantry, Dec. 24. 1864, at Almont, for 1 year, age 20. Mustered in Dec. 30, 1864. Mustered out at Detroit, Mich., June 30, 1865.

**Spencer, Oscar**, Enlisted in company D, Thirtieth Infantry, Dec. 10, 1864. At Almont, for 1 year, age 27. Mustered in Dec. 30, 1864, Corporal Jan. 4, 1865. Mustered out at Detroit, Mich., June 30, 1865.

**Warren, Charles P.,** Enlisted in company B, Thirtieth Infantry, Dec. 12, 1864, at Almont, for 1 year, age 26. Mustered in Dec. 13. 1864. Mustered out at Detroit, Mich.. June 30, 1865.

**Way, Loan, or Lan**, Enlisted in company B, Thirtieth Infantry, Dec. 15, 1864, at Almont, for 1 year, age 18. Mustered in Dec. 15, 1864. Mustered out at Detroit, Mich., June 30, 1865.

**Whitcomb, Alonzo,** Enlisted in company B, Thirtieth Infantry, Dec. 8, 1864, at Almont, for 1 year, age 26. Mustered in Dec. 13, 1864. Mustered out at Detroit, Mich., June 30, 1865.

**Woodman, William W.**, Enlisted in company B, Thirtieth Infantry, Dec. 10, 1864, at Almont, for 1 year, age 18. Mustered in Dec. 13, 1864. Mustered out at Detroit, Mich., June 30, 1865.

## *1st Colored Infantry*

**Francis, Abram**, Enlisted in company D, First Colored Infantry, Feb. 12. 1864. at Almont, for 3 years, age 33. Mustered in Feb. 17. 1864. Deserted at Detroit, Mich., March 25, 1864.

## *1st Michigan Engineers and Mechanics*

**Gourlay, Robert**, Enlisted in company L, Engineers and Mechanics, Jan. 12, 1863, at Almont, for 3 years, age 43. Mustered in Feb. 27, 1864. Discharged at Detroit, Mich., Aug. 17, 1865.

## *1st Michigan Light Artillery*

**Martin, Hiram B.**, Almont. Enlisted in Battery B. Dec. 4, 1861. at Port Huron, for 3 years, age 31. Mustered in Dec. 16, 1861. Transferred as First Sergeant to Battery A May 26, 1863.

**Ingham, Chauncey**, Almont. Enlisted in Battery C, Dec. 15. 1861. at Grand Rapids, for 3 years, age 21. Mustered in Dec. 18, 1861. Re-enlisted Dec. 28, 1863, at Prospect, Tenn. Mustered in Jan. 1, 1864. Mustered out at Detroit, Mich., June 22, 1865.

**Ingham, Joseph**, Almont. Enlisted in Battery C, Dec. 3, 1861, at Grand Rapids, for 3 years, age 39. Mustered in Dec. 18, 1861. Discharged for disability at Detroit, Mich., July 22, 1862.

*Acknowledgements*

**The author wishes to thank the following in no particular order. Without all of them, this book could not have been written:**

John Heiser, Gettysburg National Military Park, Library and Research Center; Gail Moreau, Detroit researcher; Bruce and Judy Kefgen, Almont researchers; Dick Webb, information on Pvt. Norvell Churchill and Forward writer; Norm Hamilton, Almont, information on Dr. William B. Hamilton; Justin Demo and Don Justin for information on the Justin brothers of St. Clair County; Tom Wearing, Tri-City Times (Imlay City, Michigan); Don and Lois Harvey for their many years of tireless research and their invaluable web site, www. michiganinthewar.org the staff of the Almont District Library, the Almont Historical Society; the Lapeer County Historical Society; the Lapeer County Genealogical Society; the Ruth Hughes Memorial Library, Imlay City, Michigan; the Michigan State Archives, Lansing; the National Archives and Records Center, Washington, D.C. and College Park, Maryland; the Detroit Public Library; the Bentley Library, University of Michigan, Ann Arbor; the Hathi Trust Digital Library; Glenn Smith; Frank Johnson; Bobby Bermudez; Ken Giorlando; Richard Faust; Harvey Hirsch; Susan Bays; Wikipedia; Ancestry.com; Charles Mauro, author; Doug Wertman, editor and Civil War expert and, of course, my perfect bride, Sue, for caring, proofreading, suggestions, etc. and my cat, Tiger, who often meowed encouragement as I wrote.

# *Sources*

*Almont Herald*, The

*Almont Times-Herald*, The

Bak, Richard. *A Distant Thunder: Michigan in the Civil War,* Huron River Press, Ann Arbor, Michigan, 2004

Bowman, Hildamae Waltz  *Almont: The Tale of Then and Now,* 1985

Casamer, Douglas M.  *The History of the Michigan Twenty-Second Infantry and the Men who Served,* 2006

Conway, James and Jamroz, David F. *Detroit's Historic Fort Wayne,* Arcadia Publishing, Charleston, S.C., 2007

Cooper, William J.  *Jefferson Davis, American,* Vintage Books, 2001

Crawford, Kim. *The 16ᵗʰ Michigan Infantry,* Morningside Books, Dayton, Ohio, 2002

*Detroit Advertiser and Tribune*, The

*Detroit Daily Advertiser*, The

*Detroit Free Press,* The

*Detroit News*, The

Ellis, Helen H. *Michigan in the Civil War: A guide to the Material in Detroit Newspapers 1861-1866*, Michigan Civil War Centennial Observance Commission, 1965

Family of Norvell Churchill

Family of William B. Hamilton

Family of the Justin brothers

Harvey, Don and Lois of www.michiganinthewar.org.org

Hamilton, Richard L. *Oh, Hast Thou Forgotten; Michigan Cavalry in the Civil War: The Gettysburg Campaign,* 2007

Hews, Fletcher W.  *History of the Formation, Movements, Camps, Scouts and Battles of The Tenth Regiment Michigan Volunteer Infantry,* John Slater's Book and Job Printing Establishment, 1864

*History of Lapeer County Michigan,* W.R. Page and Co., Chicago, 1881

Husby, Karla Jean and Wittenberg, Eric J. (editors), *Under Custer's Command: The Civil War Journal of James Henry Avery,* Brassey's, Washington, D.C., 2000

Hutchins, Richard G. *Fowlerville Goes to War 1861-1865*, Self-published

Hutton, Paul Andrew (editor), *The Custer Reader,* University of Oklahoma Press, 2004 edition

Kidd, J.H. *A Cavalryman with Custer,* Bantam Books edition, New York, 1991

LaFantasie, Glenn W. *Twilight at Little Round Top: July 2, 1863 – The Tide Turns at Gettysburg,* First Vintage Civil War Library edition, October, 2007

*Lapeer County (MI) Press*, The

Longacre, Edward G. *The Cavalry at Gettysburg: A Tactical Study of Mounted Operations During the Civil War's Pivotal Campaign, 9 June – 14 July 1863,* University of Nebraska Press, 1986

Longacre, Edward G. *Custer and His Wolverines: The Michigan Cavalry Brigade 1861-1865,* Combined Publishing, Conshohocken, PA 1997

Mason, Philip P. and Pentecost, Paul J. *From Bull Run to Appomattox: Michigan's Role in the Civil War,* Wayne State University Press, Detroit, 1961

*Michigan History Magazine  Michigan and the Civil War: An Anthology,* 1999

*Michigan History Magazine, Thank God for Michigan!* 1998

Michigan Publishing Company, *Michigan Poets and Poetry,* 1904

Mitchell, Robert E. The Organizational Performance of Michigan's Adjutant General and the Federal Provost Marshal in Recruiting Michigan's Boys in Blue, *Michigan Historical Review*, Volume 28, 2002

National Archives and Records Administration, Washington, D.C. and College Park, MD

Poremba, David Lee (editor) *If I Am Found Dead: Michigan Voices from the Civil War,* Ann Arbor (MI) Media Group, L.L.C., 2006

Sridharan, Susan, editor *History of the 22nd Michigan*

Turner, George H. (Assistant Adjutant General of Michigan) *Record of Service of Michigan Volunteers in the Civil War 1861-1865,* 46 volumes, Ihling Bros. and Everard, Kalamazoo, Michigan, 1900

Wert, Jeffry D. *From Winchester to Cedar Creek: The Shenandoah Campaign of 1864,* Stackpole Books, 1997 edition

Wikipedia

Williams, Frederick D. *Michigan Soldiers in the Civil War,* 5th edition, Michigan Historical Center, 2002

Wittenberg, Eric J. *Plenty of Blame to Go Around: Jeb Stuart's Controversial Ride to Gettysburg,* Savas Beatie, L.L.C., 2006

Wittenberg, Eric J. Petruzzi, David and Nugent, Michael F. *One Continuous Fight: The Retreat from Gettysburg and the Pursuit of Lee's Army of Northern Virginia, July 4 – 14, 1863,* Savas Beatie L.L.C., 2008

Woodford, Frank B. *Father Abraham's Children: Michigan Episodes in the Civil War,* Wayne State University Press, Detroit, 1961

# INDEX

Hogan, Andrew  64, 133, 144

Hollenbeck, Sarah  110

Hooker, Joseph  34, 96

Hopkins, John  27

Horan, Patrick  160

Hough, John B.  28, 127

Howe, Lorenzo M.  152

Howe, Samuel R.  133, 152

Hull, Henry160

Hull, Mylon  152

Hull, William  17

Humphrey, Alonzo A.  173

Hunt, James  137

Ingham, Chauncey  178

Ingham, Joseph  178

Irving. George W.  137

Ives, Edward H.  138

Ives, Isaac  153

Jackson, Thomas "Stonewall" 50, 60

James, George K.  161

Jaxon, Peter  28

Jefferson, Thomas  17, 48

Jenness, Ellen F.  75

Jerome, David  14

Johnson, Andrew  81. 82

Johnston, Benjamin F.  64-68, 127, 146

Johnston, Betsy Ann  67

Jones, William  142

Justin, Alonzo Lee Jr. 119, 120, 121

Justin, Alonzo Lee Sr.  110

Justin, Bertha  116

Justin, Charles  110

Justin,  Clark O.  110, 121, 122, 123

Justin, Cora  116

Justin, Don  110

Justin, Dorah  116

Justin, Ella  116

Justin, Ellen Ervin  116

Justin, Emily Dunton  123

Justin, Estella  116

Justin, Esther  116

Justin, Fannie Gardner  122

Justin, George  123, 124

Justin, Gershum  110

Justin, Isaac  117, 118

Justin, Jimmie  116

Justin, John  110, 116

Justin, Margaret  116

Justin, Maria  118

Justin, Mary Redfield  118

Justin, Ralph  110, 123

Justin, Sarah Ann  116

## *About the Author*

Richard Paul (Rick) Liblong is a Michiganian, having lived in the state for nearly a half century, even though he now lives in Virginia with his wife, Sue. Rick is passionate about and has studied Michigan and American history since childhood and after reading a special edition of *Michigan History* magazine entitled "Thank God for Michigan!" he decided to tell the stories of some of the men from rural Michigan in the Civil War and used his hometown of Almont and Lapeer County as an example.

Rick holds a communications degree from Michigan State University and served as a communications manager for The Dow Chemical Company, as Communications Director for a United States Senator and as Public Affairs Director for a U.S. Government agency.

He was named an "Outstanding Alumni in the Department of Communication Arts and Sciences" at Michigan State University in 2008. In recent years, he has been a writer and consultant. He began his writing career at *The Almont Times-Herald* in the early 1960's.

He is the author of numerous articles published in *Michigan History* as well as many other newspapers and magazines.